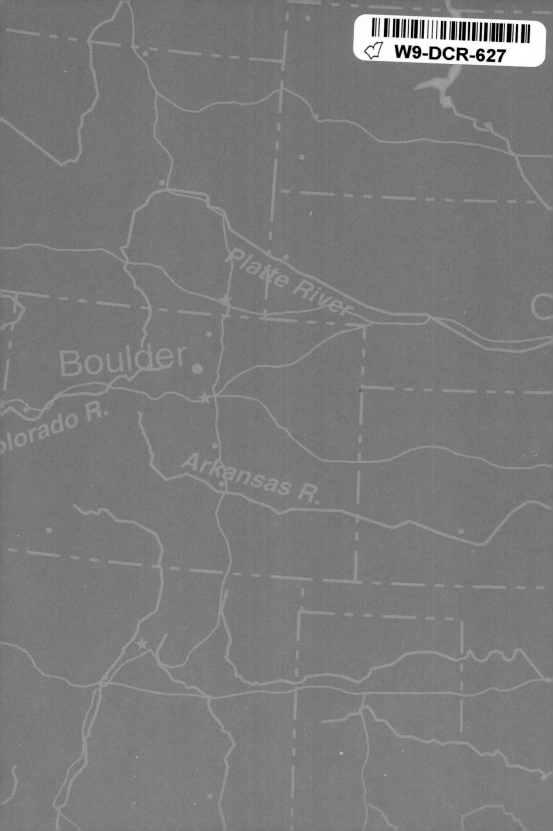

Smooth Rolling
RV Care, Safety & Performance

The Good Sam Club
Essential RVers Collection

Credits

Interior Design: Bill Nelson Creative, Inc.
Cover Design: FraneyDesign

ISBN 0-934798-64-8   (hardcover)

Smooth Rolling: RV Care, Safety & Performance draws from individual titles from TL Enterprises: *The RV Handbook* by Bill Estes, illustrated by Miyaki Illustration; *10- Minute Tech* by the Editors of Trailer Life Books, illustrated by Bill Tipton and *The Good Sam RV Cookbook* by Beverly Edwards.

Cover Photos: *(Top right)*: Courtesy of Winnebago Industries, Forest City, IA 50436 (515) 582-3535, http://www.winnebagoind.com
(Top left): Digital Imagery, copyright ©1999 PhotoDisk, Inc.
(Bottom right): copyright ©2000 Michael Banks/Stone

Printed in the U.S.A. (0400)

Table of Contents

Introduction

"Smooth Rolling" is the farewell wish for all RVers as they head out on the road. We want all trips to be predictable and safe. But are you sure you'll be able to deal with the small bumps along the way? Do you know the best way to deal with an overheated engine? What happens when diesel engines flood? Can you mix radial and bias-ply tires? How best to handle driving around curves? How can you maximize fuel economy?

In this book, you'll find answers to the most-asked questions about RV weight and handling, towing safety and engines, their systems and tires. Chapters include useful ideas for: trailer backing and braking, proper hitch adjustment, handling the weight of your rig safely in crosswinds, making tires last longer, good start-up and driving habits, and troubleshooting when engines won't start.

Because your RV is a big investment in time and money, you'll want to know everything you can do to keep it running smooth and hassle-free. *Smooth Rolling: RV Care, Safety & Performance* offers up-to-date information in an easy-to-understand style so you'll be able to weigh your options and make the right decisions to keep you rolling along.

Be sure to check out the bonus chapter at the end of the book featuring delicious appetizer recipes from fellow Good Sam Members!

Weight, Handling, and Safety

In this chapter the following items will be covered:

- Mirrors and Visibility
- Vehicle Size
- Trailer Backing
- Braking and Brake Fade
- Loading and Load Ratings
- Weighing a Vehicle
- Tow Vehicle/Trailer Matching

By nature, most RVs are larger and bulkier than the family sedan and cannot be expected to handle the same way. In particular, towing a trailer requires new skills and judgment because a tow vehicle/trailer combination is an articulated vehicle, that is, segmented or joined.

New criteria and some adjustments in driving habits are necessary to graduate from a car or truck to an articulated vehicle or a motorhome. It isn't difficult, and few problems occur unless a driver fails to realize that tow vehicles and motorhomes aren't as agile or as powerful as cars and light trucks alone. What's more, violation of their weight limits can have serious consequences.

The major factors that must be considered for safe RVing include:

- Visibility—forward and side- and rear-view mirrors
- The vehicle's length, width, and height
- Turning circle
- How the vehicle tracks while turning
- Braking ability
- Stability during emergency maneuvers
- Stability on curves
- Stability in crosswinds
- Acceleration for passing
- Loading and load ratings
- Weight distribution

MIRRORS AND VISIBILITY

Good forward and side visibility are needed in any motor vehicle, particularly in one that is larger and more difficult to handle than a typical car or truck alone. The levels of visibility we tend to accept as adequate may not be very good; visibility often can be improved.

Few vehicles have poor forward visibility even though some may have relatively small windshields that restrict the upward scenic view. In motorhomes, side vision sometimes is restricted by excessively large corner posts between the windshield and the side windows and by mirrors that are positioned too high. Little can be done about corner posts after the fact, but it's a point of consideration while shopping for a new unit. Side visibility in motorhomes may be restricted by

Figure 1.1: The view through side-mounted mirrors sometimes is partially blocked, requiring repositioning.

window frames—particularly those that block the view through mirrors *(Figure 1.1)*. The solution is either to move the mirror to a more advantageous position or to modify the side window. Moving the mirror usually is the easiest solution.

Figure 1.2: Stick-on convex mirrors can help eliminate a "blind spot" to the right rear of the vehicle.

Mirrors themselves are an area of poor visibility, which can lead to accidents. Mirrors on a tow vehicle or motorhome should be 10 × 7 inches to offer an adequate field of vision. On tow vehicles, door-mount positions are far better than fender mounts. Fender-mounted mirrors don't offer a good rear view due to their size and their distance from the driver. Also, a convex right-side mirror, which helps the driver monitor his or her "blind spot," cannot be used as a fender mount. The solution for cars is a set of good door-mounted mirrors, with a convex mirror added on the right side. On trucks and vans, extensions may be used to move some mirror heads outward, or a replacement set of extended mirrors may be purchased. Extensions and replacement mirrors are available at RV supply stores.

While trucks, vans, and motorhomes usually have larger mirror heads, the owner still must make sure visibility is not restricted by window frames or by an insecure mirror mounting that causes excessive vibration, blurring the reflected images. Most right-side mirrors of pickup trucks and vans do not have wide-angle lenses, which must be added to the face of the mirror *(Figure 1.2)*. On motorhomes, the side-mounted mirror often is about two-third conventional view and one-third wide angle *(Figure 1.3)*. This combination is acceptable but tends to restrict the driver's ability to see the area around the rear tires, which is helpful to keep from running over curbs while making tight turns, as well as checking for exhaust smoke or an errant wheel cover. The preferred arrangement is a convex mirror that is outside the conventional mirror. Add-on convex mirrors are available at RV supply and stores that sell equipment to truckers, positioned immediately below or above the primary mirror *(Figure 1.4)*. The preferred location is the one that offers maximum visibility.

Figure 1.3: Large motorhome mirrors offer excellent combination of conventional lens with adjustable convex lens.

Figure 1.4: A convex lens may be attached to the frame so it does not block the lens of a conventional towing mirror.

TIPS THAT WORK

Be a Flasher

Glare and bright sunlight can often obscure an RV's flashing turn signals from other drivers. Those vehicles traveling alongside a large rig may not have any warning at all that you're planning a lane change.

Adding auxiliary signal lights to the outside mirror brackets can help overcome such deficiencies. Toward this end, the mirror-mounted turn signal lights used on large semi-tractors are readily available, but are probably a bit bulky for most motorhomes and tow vehicles. Fabricating your own light kit is simple.

Smaller lights that are more in proportion to your rig can be chosen from the array of RV marker lights sold by RV and automotive-supply stores. You'll need four: two red and two amber.

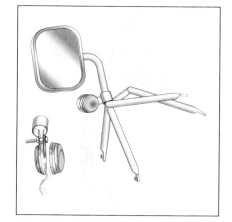

Next you'll need to obtain two $6 \times 1 \times \frac{1}{16}$- inch aluminum strips. These will be formed into brackets to hold the marker lights. Several feet of 16-gauge automotive wire, electrical tape, rubber grommets, and six machine screws with nuts (sizes 6-32) will also be needed to complete the project. Some vehicles may also need a heavy-duty turn signal flasher.

Form the aluminum strips around each mirror bracket, and drill for one machine screw. Drill the opposite end to match the mounting holes in the marker lights you've selected, and assemble the lights with the red lens facing to the rear of the RV. Certain marker lights may require minor modifications to make them fit flush on the aluminum bracket.

Make the bracket holes slightly smaller than the attaching screw since the lights will need good metal-to-metal contact at this point to be properly grounded.

With this complete, you can now decide whether to run the power wire outside the RV's mirror bracket tube, or drill the ends of the bracket and route the wire internally.

Regardless of the method you choose, the next step requires drilling the vehicle door and side wall to provide a path for the power wire to reach the vehicle's turn-signal circuit. Be sure to install rubber grommets at all locations where the wire passes through bare metal. Depending upon which is easiest, you can tap into the RV's sidelight marker (if it flashes during turns) or the front signal.

Solder and tape all electrical connections. Use a small bead of silicone sealer to weatherproof the seam between the two marker lights, and you're done.

Your next trip should prove the value of your mirror-mounted flashers, because more drivers will see and react to your signaled intentions.

Leon Boeck, Easton, MN

VEHICLE SIZE

Most of us drive passenger cars or light trucks more frequently and graduate to our RVs only occasionally. Thus, it's always necessary to make a mental transition and keep the size and handling characteristics of the larger rig in mind. Failing to do so may result in a tendency to make turns too tightly, run over curbs, hit stationary objects, or crowd other traffic. It may take some concentration for the novice RV owner, but acclimation happens fairly rapidly. The get-acquainted period may be difficult to get through without minor dings and scrapes, but traffic accidents are unusual, even though the new driver may not have fully adjusted to the particular characteristics of handling an RV.

The best defense against problems associated with the vehicle's size is practice. All too often, we encounter a tight turn into or out of a campground site or service station and are tentative about our ability to make the turn. Practicing tight maneuvers will improve our judgment, reducing the chance of embarrassing situations. Practice also helps improve our judgment in making sure we don't hit overhanging tree limbs and other such obstacles. It's helpful to measure the actual height of the vehicle and list this figure somewhere on the dash for reference when driving under structures that are marked for road clearance. If you're uncomfortable driving under unmarked overhangs, exit the vehicle and check clearance if the situation permits. Soon you'll have a clearer mental picture of your RV's height.

Tailswing is an RV handling characteristic that causes quite a number of dings and scrapes. It occurs during tight, slow-speed maneuvers when the rear of a trailer or motorhome swings opposite the direction you are steering *(Figure 1.5)* Tailswing can be monitored in the mirrors of a motorhome or truck camper, allowing you to avoid costly conflicts with lampposts and other obstacles. But with a tow vehicle and trailer, you're blind on the right side during left turns. Also, while backing to the left, we can see where we're going on that side, but we can't see the right side of the trailer. Pulling forward sharply to the left and then straightening the wheel can swing the trailer's rear to the right—into a post, tree, or other obstacle if it happens to be your misfortune. The best defense is to practice in a parking lot and observe how the vehicle's rear changes position. With a tow vehicle and trailer, have someone else drive while you watch what happens in tight turns.

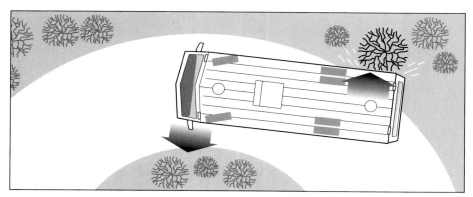

Figure 1.5: Tailswing creates the danger of a collision when the rear of a motorhome or trailer swings in the opposite direction of the turn.

On-the-Road Performance

RVs are like most other vehicles that are larger and heavier than cars and light trucks in that they must be driven differently. We can't expect to pass other vehicles with the same authority in a 16,000-pound motorhome as we do a car. However, it is possible to pass. Drivers of 18-wheelers do it, but they wait for enough clear highway.

While passing, don't hesitate to use the full rpm potential of your engine when necessary. This means holding the accelerator pedal to the floor, causing the automatic transmission to downshift and allowing it to determine the upshift point. With V-8 engines, the transmission is programmed to upshift at 4,000 to 4,500 rpm, depending on the engine; these levels are not excessive in short bursts.

Road Manners

RVs are heavier than cars, and they climb hills more slowly than other private passenger traffic, as do 18-wheelers. But fast traffic seems more tolerant of slow 18-wheelers than of slow recreational travelers, which makes courtesy an important safety factor. It's best to frequently monitor rear-view mirrors and be aware of vehicles behind us. When a vehicle is tailgating and trying to pass, drive slightly to the right to give the other driver a better view of the road ahead, even if a passing opportunity does not exist at the time. Use turnouts when possible, and don't follow another vehicle so closely that the vehicle passing you cannot return to your lane. Failure to display courtesy to other drivers can affect your own safety by causing angry reactions and poor judgment in other motorists.

Maneuvering

While all RV drivers must acclimate themselves to longer vehicles that require more care while maneuvering, some RVs track differently than others in turns. With the exception of very large motorhomes, all the self-propelled RVs are relatively easy to handle in turns. With the large ones, the driver must take extra care to swing as wide as possible in tight turns. The techniques are to keep the vehicle as far away from obstacles as possible, and proceed as far as possible into the area of a turn before beginning the turn.

Trailers require more practice and more visualizing because it's necessary to learn how the tow vehicle and trailer respond to steering input. Small- to medium-length travel trailers will follow closely in the tracks of the tow vehicle in turns, so the tow vehicle needn't be steered exceptionally wide in turns. A long travel trailer will track moderately on the inside of the turn, requiring more space. A fifth-wheel trailer tracks considerably farther to the inside of the turn *(Figure 1.6)*, so a turn that is not taken rather wide will result in the trailer's tires climbing a curb. The reason for this is that a fifth-wheel trailer's hitch point is directly above the rear axle of the tow vehicle, whereas the pivot point of a travel trailer is four to five feet behind the tow vehicle's rear bumper. The tow vehicle's tailswing tends to make a travel trailer follow closely in the tow vehicle's tracks. But tow-vehicle tailswing does not steer a fifth-wheel trailer, so it tracks farther to the inside of the turn. As fifth-wheel trailer length increases, more care must be taken during turns.

Figure 1.6: Ball-type trailers track closely with the tow vehicle but fifth-wheelers track to the inside of the turn.

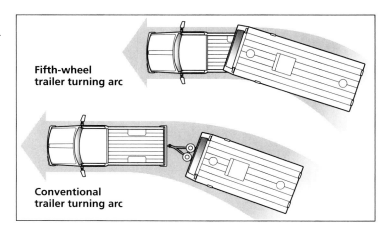

Fifth-wheel
trailer turning arc

Conventional
trailer turning arc

TRAILER BACKING

With conventionally hitched trailers, ease of backing increases with trailer length, which the opposite of what most novices often assume. A utility trailer is much more difficult to back; its short ball-to-axle distance causes it to react swiftly to tow-vehicle steering input, while a longer trailer will react gradually. Fifth-wheel trailers are more difficult to back than conventional trailers, requiring more practice. Techniques for backing differ widely.

Here are some general guidelines for backing all types of trailers:

- When you are ready to begin backing, place your hand at the bottom of the steering wheel. Then move it in the direction you want your trailer to go *(Figure 1.7)*. This is more effective with conventional trailers than with fifth-wheelers, which require more turning of the steering wheel.
- Hand-held CB radios, available at low cost, can allow an assistant to relay backing instructions to the driver more effectively.
- After arriving at a site, inspect it for the final position of the trailer and lay a length of white cord (clothesline) along the intended path. Begin laying the line a few inches to the left of where you want the left rear wheel of the trailer to be. Lay the line out to

Figure 1.7:
While backing a trailer, steer from the bottom of the wheel and turn in the direction you want the trailer to go.

about where the left front of the tow vehicle will be when the trailer is in position, and continue with the line along the intended backing path so the line can be seen in the left rear-view mirror. Backing to the left is easiest, but this method can also help while backing to the right.

Backing Fifth-Wheels

When backing fifth-wheels, follow these procedures:

- Watch your outside mirrors and when you see the trailer moving where you don't want it to go, turn the steering wheel in that direction. For example, while looking in the left mirror, if you see

TIPS THAT WORK

Glare-Free Backing

When arriving at a campsite at night, the task of backing into an unknown spot is made more difficult by the reflection of your tow vehicle's backup lights off the front of the trailer. The offending lights can be extinguished during these times with the installation of a switch in the backup-light circuit of the tow rig.

The switch can be purchased at any auto-parts store. The type you select depends only on your personal preferences. There are SPST toggle and rocker versions that work equally well.

The wire leading to the backup lights is usually attached to the reverse switch near the base of the steering column under the dash or on the transmission under the vehicle. Find this wire, and verify it with a test light by operating the backup lights. Then cut the wire, and splice the wires running from the new switch into the circuit at this location.

I put my backup-light kill switch beside the electric brake controller, which I have mounted under the dash. It could, however, be located in any convenient spot near the driver.

Andy L. Hughes
Rustin, LA

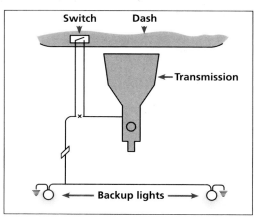

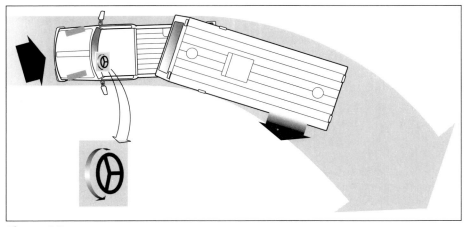

Figure 1.8: If a fifth-wheel trailer moves in an undesirable direction while backing, turn the steering wheel in that direction to straighten out.

the trailer moving toward that side and you don't want it to go in that direction, turn the wheel to the left *(Figure 1.8)*. Position someone near the rear of the trailer, in the driver's view, to watch for obstructions.

- Remember that you have no tailswing leverage to help you steer the fifth-wheeler while backing, as one has with a conventionally hitched trailer. Therefore, the tow vehicle must be at a significant angle to the trailer before any turning occurs. This does not necessarily mean that extreme winding of the steering wheel is required, but it does mean that turns must be started before you get to the slot into which you're trying to move. The trick is figuring how much earlier. Each time you pull out of a slot, observe the path the trailer wheels make, and pay particular attention to the surprisingly long way you go before the trailer is aligned straight behind the tow vehicle. That is the magical point at which you should start to turn if you were to reverse the process and back into that slot.

Backing All Types of RVs

Before backing an RV, be sure to inspect the site, decide where you want the wheels to be, and lay a line of white cord or place "targets" on the ground—small rocks, pieces of wood, and such—along the path that the wheels must follow to end up where you want them. When the wheels are directly opposite the target, they serve as guides not to back up too far.

No matter what the type of rig, practice is the answer. Regardless of the techniques the driver and his or her helper may use, there is no substitute for repetition of backing maneuvers until they become almost second nature.

BRAKING AND BRAKE FADE

While RV brakes are adequate for most situations, care is necessary to avoid overheating, which can lead to brake fade. When brakes fade, friction has raised the temperature of brake pads and linings to extremely high levels, resulting in temporary loss of braking. The brake pedal is still firm, and its height is normal, but heavy foot pressure on the pedal produces little or no braking action. This is a frightening situation, caused by excessive use of brakes to retard downhill speeds on long, mountain grades. Beyond use of top-quality brake components, the cure is prevention—downshifting to a gear range that is low enough to retard speed sufficiently that brakes need not be used more than occasionally. This way, enough braking performance is reserved to make an emergency stop if it becomes necessary.

The proper way to use brakes is to apply them intermittently, with moderate pressure, to scrub off speed. Then release the pedal to allow the brakes to cool. Do not ride the brake pedal for long periods.

If brakes fade prematurely—which means an emergency stop cannot be made effectively on level highway even though brakes have not been preheated—or if braking is not sufficient for more than moderate reduction of speed on a downhill grade, the brake system should be checked for glazed brake pads and linings. Top-quality semi-metallic brake pads and linings should be used.

When a trailer is involved, action of the electric trailer brakes should be apparent to the driver and sufficient to take care of the trailer. The controller should be adjusted so maximum braking action does not cause trailer-wheel lockup. If the driver can not feel the action of the trailer brakes, he or she has no way of monitoring whether or not they're functional.

Figure 1.9 Labeling rules require RV manufacturers to post specific weight definitions to help owners prevent overloading.

Many RVs have relatively high centers of gravity, which complicate the use of brakes while traveling curving roads. By staging test situations, it should be possible to determine the vehicle's response to braking action on curves. Handling deficiencies such as a tendency toward excessive body roll (lean) can be exaggerated while using brakes. You should practice using brakes in situations other than straight-ahead driving so you will know what to expect. Handling deficiencies may be caused by weight imbalance, overloading, or poor shock absorbers. An RV whose handling is difficult to improve due to design deficiencies must be driven at slower speeds to allow reaction time in emergency situations.

LOADING AND LOAD RATINGS

RVs are subject to overloading and the problems that result from it. They include:

- Improper handling
- Lengthened stopping distance
- Increased wear on brakes
- Reduced acceleration capability
- Reduced service life of components such as wheel bearings and springs
- Component failures, primarily tires (see Chapter 2)

Tire failures can lead directly to accidents, so it behooves every RV owner to become educated about weight and weight distribution and to take action by applying the knowledge to his or her specific situation.

Several items contribute to weight problems:

- Insufficient load capacity built into the vehicles by their manufacturers to reasonably cover the amount of weight owner will add
- Insufficient information distributed by manufacturers and dealers about the importance of weight and loading
- Lack of motivation by RV owners to acquire information (available in magazines and in books) they need to avoid overloading

All vehicles have load ratings, which determine how much weight (carrying capacity) the owner can add. The amount of information available to the consumer changed substantially in late 1996 when a weight labeling program introduced by the Recreational Vehicle Industry Association (RVIA) went into effect. At that time, the RVIA began requiring their members to affix labels featuring this information to all their units (Figure 1.9).

Prior to late 1996, labels included only load ratings, with no additional information offered on actual weight of the vehicle. Although the new label allows the manufacturer to list "approximate" weight of the RV, it is far more detailed than the information previously offered, and it gives the owner specific limits on the weight of supplies and equipment that can be carried on trips.

Any RV can be overloaded, but travel trailers tend to be less susceptible because they don't have voluminous exterior storage capacity; camping equipment, tools, and other supplies usually are hauled in the tow vehicle.

Fifth-wheel trailers have more storage capacity, and their owners frequently travel for longer periods, hence the tendency to carry more supplies and equipment. Motorhomes have the greatest potential for overloading because of their "basement" storage compartments.

Unfortunately few RV owners bother to weigh their vehicles, so they do not discover overload situations that can lead to tire blowouts, bearing failures and, in severe cases, wheel breakage. Also, overloading usually causes spring sag, poor handling, and inadequate braking.

WEIGHT RATINGS AND DESCRIPTIONS

Gross Vehicle Weight Rating (GVWR) The maximum weight of the vehicle and all its contents, including passengers—i.e., the maximum to which the vehicle can be loaded

Unloaded Vehicle Weight (UVW) Weight of the RV including factory-installed options, with full LP-gas tank or cylinders. Does not include gasoline or diesel fuel, fresh water, or accessories installed by the dealer

Net Carrying Capacity (NCC) Maximum weight of all passengers (if applicable), personal belongings, food, fresh water, supplies—derived by subtracting the UVW from the GVWR

Gross Axle Weight Rating (GAWR) The maximum to which the specific axle can be loaded

Gross Combination Weight Rating (GCWR) The maximum permissible weight of the vehicle and trailer (or motorhome and "dinghy" vehicle) with all passengers, fluids, and supplies

Dry Weight (DW) The manufacturer's listing of the approximate weight of an RV with no supplies, water, fuel, or passengers

Wet Weight (WW) Weight of an actual RV (as listed in *Trailer Life* or *MotorHome* magazines) with full fuel and water tanks but no supplies or passengers

TIPS THAT WORK

RV Weight Watcher

In the event that you have trouble locating a public scale, here is a relatively simple do-it-yourself method for determining trailer-tongue weight. All that is required is a 0- to 300-pound bathroom scale, two pieces of 1-inch pipe (approximately 8 inches long), one 4-foot section of 4 × 4-inch lumber, and a wood block that is the same height as the scale.

With these items placed in accordance with the diagram, the trailer's tongue weight can be calculated by multiplying the scale reading by three. (Example: a scale reading of 200 × 3 = 600 pounds hitch weight.) Note that the maximum weight measurable by this equipment is 900 pounds. To obtain an accurate reading, both the trailer and the 4 × 4 beam must be level.

James Brown, Yardley, PA

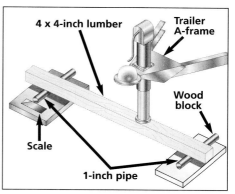

4 x 4-inch lumber

Trailer A-frame

Wood block

Scale

1-inch pipe

WEIGHING A VEHICLE

Owners of RVs built prior to the use of the new RVIA weight-label may not feel the need to weigh their units, although the word "approximate" in the listing suggests that it's a wise move anyway. Owners of RVs built prior to the introduction of the label should acquire weight figures that will enable them to stay within load limits. The following weighing procedures should be used:

1. Locate the manufacturer's identification sticker or plate for future reference. On cars and trucks it will be on the driver's door pillar; on motorhomes it usually is inside, near the driver's seat, or just inside the door; on trailers it's usually on the left front exterior.

2. Weigh the vehicle while loaded for a trip. If the vehicle is a motorhome, camping van, or truck camper, weigh each wheel if you can find an axle scale or a wheel scale. In absence of such a scale, a platform scale will suffice, although it's not sufficiently

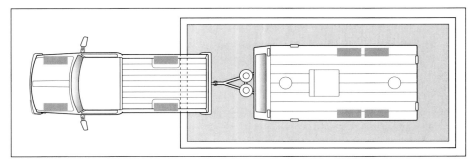

Figure 1.10: To determine a trailer's axle weight, position the trailer wheels on the scale and the tow vehicle rear wheels immediately off the scale.

accurate to measure individual wheel weights. If you must use a platform scale, weigh the vehicle five times: gross weight, front axle, rear axle, left side, right side. If the vehicle cannot be loaded for a trip, estimate the amount of weight you will add so you can determine if an overload condition might occur.

If you are weighing a trailer, get two figures: trailer wheels only (hitched to the tow vehicle, (with tow vehicle off scale) and gross trailer weight (trailer unhitched from tow vehicle).

3. Compare your weight figures with the manufacturer's load ratings and with the ratings stamped on the sidewalls of your tires. The weight of your loaded vehicle should not exceed the GVWR, either of the GAWRs, or the individual ratings on your tires. The reason multiple weight readings are necessary is that improper weight distribution may overload an individual tire or set of dual tires even though the GVWR has not been violated.

Finding and Using Scales

Platform or wheel scales can be found at equipment-rental yards, moving companies, grain elevators, and other such establishments. Check the Yellow Pages of your phone book under Scales, Weighers, Weight, or Weighing. Using a scale is a simple procedure, but one very important procedure must be observed: **The vehicle being weighed must be level.** All platform scales are flat, but the aprons surrounding them may not be. When the aprons are not level, the RV must be positioned so it is level even though one side or one end may be off the scale. Leveling blocks or boards may be needed.

Position the trailer wheels on the scale for a weight reading with the tow vehicle hitched to the trailer but off the scale *(Figure 1.10)*. This is the figure you will use to determine if axle or tire load ratings are violated. Unhitch the trailer on the scale (vehicle off scale) to determine the trailer's gross weight.

Substantial lateral imbalance with trailers is unusual, which in most cases eliminates the need to weigh each side of the trailer. The exception would be a situation in which weighing the trailer's axle(s) indicates that weight is near or over the tire ratings. In that case, weighing each side of the trailer is advisable to make sure the heavy side is not above the tire maximum load ratings. If it is, reduction in weight is necessary.

In Table 1.1, the calculations determine if the weight carried by four 205/75R15ST load range C tires rated at 1,820 pounds each at 50 psi is in excess of the tire load ratings. The result: Tire capacity is in excess of the actual load—a safe situation.

Table 1.1:
Weight ratings and actual weights of a 26-foot travel trailer

Manufacturer's Weight Ratings

GAWR, front axle	3,500 lbs.
GAWR, rear axle	3,500 lbs.
GVWR	7,000 lbs.

Wet weight
Front axle*	2,800 lbs.
Rear axle*	2,800 lbs.

Total weight on trailer tires	**5,600 lbs.**

*Weighing with trailer hitched to tow vehicle, utilizing a load-distributing hitch. Axle weights will differ when measured without the use of a load-distributing hitch.

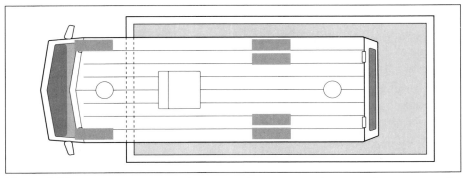

Figure 1.11: A motorhome may have an adequate carrying capacity on one axle while the other is overloaded, which can be detected by weighing each axle separately.

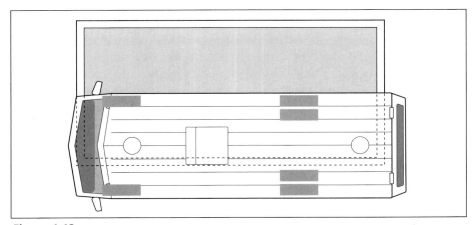

Figure 1.12: Weighing each side of a motorhome or camper can identify overloading that cannot be detected by a gross weight reading.

Although it's not necessary when evaluating tire loading, you should also measure hitch weight, which will help in evaluating the trailer's stability. Hitch weight is measured by positioning the trailer so the hitch support (tow vehicle or tongue jack) is off the scale. (Don't use spring bars of a load-distributing hitch, which will prevent an accurate hitch-weight measurement.) Weigh the trailer wheels only; subtract that figure from the trailer's gross weight to determine hitch weight.

Table 1.2:
Weight ratings and actual weights of a 32-foot Class A
motorhome

Manufacturer's Weight Ratings

GAWR, front axle	6,000 lbs.
GAWR, rear axle	11,000 lbs.
GVWR	17,000 lbs.

Wet weight
Front axle	5,380 lbs.
Rear axle	9,740 lbs.
Left side	7,700 lbs.
Right side	7,420 lbs.
Total weight	**15,120 lbs.**

Weighing a Motorhome, Truck Camper, or Van Conversion

If a wheel or axle scale is available, weigh each wheel individually. If the weights must be taken on a platform scale, weigh the entire vehicle first. Then move it fore and aft for front and rear axle weights *(Figure 1.11)*. Move it left and right to weigh each side *(Figure 1.12)*. If the apron around the scale is not level, it is essential to position the vehicle so the off-scale tires are only an inch or so outside the perimeter of the scale on a surface that is level with the scale. Or, level the coach with boards or leveling blocks. Errors will occur if the coach is not level.

The motorhome in Table 1.2 has a realistic NCC and reasonably good balance so that the owner can make use of the NCC without overloading either axle.

The tires are LT235/85R16E, rated to carry 3,042 pounds in single configuration or 2,778 pounds in dual configuration. This means 11,112 pounds of rear capacity—ample in this situation, even in view of the fact that both sets of tires rarely are loaded evenly and a margin of safety is needed to account for uneven loading.

Some motorhomes have tag axles—an add-on rear nondrive axle with single tires. These axles are designed to boost the rear GAWR and allow the coach builder to assign the motorhome a higher GVWR. Use of a tag axle, which raises the number of rear tires to six, does not change the rear-drive axle's load rating or the tire ratings. However, by supporting some of the motorhome's rear weight, rear-axle and rear-tire overloading can be avoided. To determine weight on the tag axle, weigh the coach with the tag axle off the scale and subtract that number from the motorhome's gross weight figure. Compare the readings to the manufacturer's GAWR rating and to the individual tire ratings.

Correcting an Overload

If weight figures indicate overloading, correction is necessary to assure safety. Correction is particularly important if tires are overloaded because they are subject to overheating and blowout, whereas the effect on other components may accrue more gradually. Tire load ratings usually are matched fairly closely with GAWRs, so overloading of an axle usually means tire overloading is imminent.

TOW VEHICLE/TRAILER MATCHING

When a prospective trailer buyer is attempting to select a tow vehicle, knowledge of trailer weight is necessary to make sure the tow vehicle is rated for the trailer weight. A very common error by prospective buyers who don't know the meaning of the load ratings is to assume that the GVWR is the trailer-weight figure they must deal with in selecting a vehicle with the correct towing rating. As the definitions listed earlier explain, the GVWR is not necessarily the actual trailer weight. In fact, the actual trailer weight usually is considerably less than the GVWR, depending on how the owner loads the trailer.

When selecting a new trailer, refer to the UVW rating if the trailer was built after late 1996; otherwise, add the manufacturer's dry-weight listing to your personal estimated weight of water, propane, and all supplies for an estimated actual weight of the trailer, loaded for a trip.

The important factor in selecting a new self-propelled RV is to make sure there is enough load capacity. Again, this can be accurately assessed if the vehicle is a late model with the RVIA weight label; it can be estimated for an earlier model by adding the manufacturer's listed dry weight to the weight of fuels, water, supplies, and passengers.

Proper attention paid to weights and weight ratings will pay large dividends in handling and safety, particularly as insurance against tire failure. A bonus is fewer mechanical problems and extended tire longevity.

Taking Care of Tires

In this chapter the following items will be covered:

- Load Versus Inflation Pressure
- Tire Damage You Can't See
- How to Make Tires Last Longer
- Choosing Replacement Tires
- About Wheels
- Tire Storage

*T*ires may be the weakest link in the RV owner's ultimate quest: to travel trouble-free. It's not that tires, per se, are unreliable. The problem is that their owners don't pay enough attention to the two important parameters: inflation pressure and load. And, often, they're handicapped at the outset by the RV manufacturer, who may not have built in enough weight capacity for supplies and passengers.

Underinflation and overloading are far more common than neglect of other important vehicle items such as engine oil, transmission oil, and coolant. Even owners who usually are very thorough in their maintenance procedures, covering all items including inflation pressure, may not know how much weight their tires are carrying.

Thus, tire maintenance deserves every RV owner's specific attention. Important tire and tire-related chassis points include:

- Regular monitoring of inflation pressure
- Evaluation of tire loading
- Regular tire rotation
- Periodic wheel alignment
- Good shock absorbers

Beyond actual hazards, proper maintenance can dramatically affect tire life. The combination of improper inflation and infrequent tire rotation greatly reduce tire life. This chapter will deal with these factors as well as tire design, radials versus bias-ply, wheel suitability, mixing of tires, and matching of dual rear tires.

LOAD VERSUS INFLATION PRESSURE

A tire can be inflated properly only if it is not overloaded, so it is impossible to discuss one topic without the other. Simplified maintenance of inflation pressure merely requires that the tire owner read the numbers on the tire sidewall *(Figure 2.1)* and make sure the tires are continually maintained at the prescribed level. Beyond the basics, tire loading should be considered in order to assure best possible wear rates and traction.

One of the first steps is to recognize that passenger-car tires and light-truck tires are different. When passenger-car tires are used on light trucks (only on the lesser-rated models), they are still regarded

Figure 2.1: The essential information for proper tire loading and maintenance is molded on the sidewall.

as passenger-car tires. Trailer tires are labeled ST (special trailer) and may be in either the car or light-truck category for load and inflation, according to specifications published by the Tire and Rim Association. These specifications are used by all tire manufacturers (with only minor exceptions) for the purpose of creating commonality of load ratings and inflation pressures among various brands. In the case of ST tires, the size designation identifies the category—automobile or light truck—to which the tire belongs.

Passenger-Car Tires

Most present-day car tires are designated with the letter P in front of a set of numbers (for example, P225/75R15), known as the P-metric system. The alphanumeric system preceded the P-metric system, and few tires are still manufactured under the alphanumeric system.

How to Read a P-Metric Tire

Using the following example, the elements of a P-metric tire become clear:

Example: **P225/75R15**

                                 P = passenger-car tire
                         225 = cross section width in millimeters
                           75 = aspect ratio
                              R = radial
                             15 = rim diameter in inches

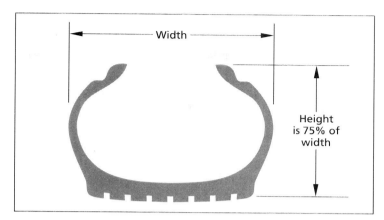

Width

Height is 75% of width

The aspect ratio is the proportion of a tire's cross-section height (from the tread to the bead seat) compared to the cross-section width (side to side). The height is 75 percent of the width of a tire that has an aspect ratio of 75 *(Figure 2.2)*.

How to Read an Alphanumeric Tire
Example: **GR78-15**

$\quad$ **G** = load capacity
$\quad$ **R** = radial
$\quad$ **78** = aspect ratio
$\quad$ **15** = rim diameter in inches

Inflation pressures molded on the sidewalls of all passenger-car tires are the maximum pressures for the maximum loads listed on the tire, and should not be exceeded. For example, the P225/75R15 is rated for 1,874 pounds maximum load at 35 psi, cold. Pressure should not exceed 35 psi, cold, under any circumstances because the tire was not designed for higher pressures. Inflation maximums for passenger-car tires are:

Standard Load (SL): 35 psi
Extra Load (XL): 41 psi

The pressure ratings are intended for use when the tires are cold; the ratings assume that higher pressures will occur while traveling due to heat buildup, and the pressure increase should not be bled off.

When a car or light truck equipped with passenger-car tires is used to tow a trailer, it's best to inflate all tires to the maximums shown on their sidewalls, which will produce the best possible towing stability.

When passenger-car tires are used on light trucks and trailers, the Tire and Rim Association recommends that load ratings be downrated to 91 percent. For example, if the tire must carry a 1,600-pound load, a tire rated for a maximum of 1,760 pounds (or thereabouts) is needed. Maximum inflation pressures shown on the tire sidewalls still apply.

Special-trailer (ST) tires that have passenger-car size designations are of the same design, except that special rubber compounds are used to reduce deterioration caused by sunlight and ozone.

Light-Truck Tires

Light-truck (LT) tires may have either the traditional numeric (for example, 7.50-16LT) or metric (LT235/75R15) identification. A typical motorhome tire would carry truck designation (LT225/70R19.5).

How to Read a Metric Light-Truck Tire

Use the following two examples to read a metric light-truck tire and a standard light-truck tire.

Example: **LT235/75R16**

LT = light-truck tire
235 = cross-section width in millimeters
75 = aspect ratio
R = radial
16 = rim diameter in inches

How to Read a Standard Light-Truck Tire
Example: **7.50R16LT**

7.50 = cross-section width in inches
R = radial
16 = rim diameter in inches
LT = light truck

Flotation Tires

Flotation-type tires have their own special category under the light-truck classification, and they're distinguished by a set of numbers beginning with the tire's overall diameter in inches.

How to Read a Flotation-type Tire
Example: **31×11.50R15LT**

31 = overall diameter in inches
11.50 = cross-section width in inches
R = radial
15 = rim diameter in inches
LT = light-truck tire

It seems logical that a partially loaded tire should be inflated accordingly. Tire manufacturers publish load and inflation tables that indicate the correct inflation pressure for a given tire load *(find these tables where tires are sold)*. This is important on light trucks and motorhomes where tire loading can differ considerably from one vehicle to another.

Different Tire Ratings

Unlike passenger car tires where the maximum inflation pressure shown on the sidewall should never be exceeded, **the pressure marked on the sidewall of a light truck or motorhome tire is the minimum pressure for the maximum load** and can be increased by 10 psi providing that the maximum inflation rating of the rim is not exceeded. The 10-psi "bonus" pressure does not increase the load-carrying capacity of the tire.

The 10 psi recommendation also applies to bias-ply tires, but additional pressure beyond the minimum for the specific load may lead to accelerated wear in the center of the tread.

The additional 10 psi above minimum-rated pressures for specific loads for light-truck tires stiffens the tire sidewall slightly, which may improve vehicle handling without a tendency to wear out the center of the tread of a radial tire. More important, it's insurance against under-inflation that can occur from the slight pressure loss that gradually occurs with all tires—loss that should be detected and corrected with frequent pressure checking but often is not.

Manufacturers of light trucks typically recommend specific pressures for the maximum load the truck is designed to carry. The ratings usually are listed in identification plates attached to the driver's side-door frame. However, light trucks usually are driven empty much of the time, and the actual load being carried by the truck is dramatically lower than the maximum load rating of the tire. Using maximum inflation when the tire is loaded far below its maximum degrades ride quality, lowers impact resistance, and reduces the size of the tire footprint. It usually will also cause accelerated wear in the center of the tread, although radial tires are minimally affected compared with bias-ply tires. Using the graduated load-inflation tables will allow you to inflate specifically to your load.

For example, an LT245/75R16 tire in D-load range is rated for 2,623 pounds load (single) at a minimum of 65 psi. In a typical situation with a pickup truck used occasionally to tow a trailer, the tire may actually be carrying about 1,200 pounds at the rear while the truck is empty. The minimum inflation pressure listed for this tire is 35 psi, rating the tire for 1,500 pounds of load.

Front tires of this same truck may be loaded to about 1,500 pounds. Adding the recommended 10 psi as a safety margin brings the appropriate inflation pressure to 45 psi for front and rear.

If a load of firewood is added to this truck while it also tows a trailer, the load on the rear tires might increase to 2,000 pounds per tire. Minimum inflation pressure for 2,000 pounds per tire is 45 psi; adding 10 psi brings the recommended pressure to 55 psi. If the tires were loaded to their maximums, correct pressure would be 75 psi, established by adding 10 psi to the 65 psi cold-inflation pressure rating appearing on the tire's sidewall.

Motorhome weights do not fluctuate widely and are usually high enough that the recommended tire pressure shown on the sidewall can be presumed appropriate if accurate weight figures are not available for the loaded motorhome. The exception may be front tires, especially on mini motorhomes. Thus, it's necessary to weigh the vehicle to determine correct tire pressures for the actual load.

Michelin's Numbers

The load and inflation ratings of most Michelin tires differ from Tire and Rim Association standards. If the load is near the maximum molded onto the tire sidewall, it's best to inflate to the pressure shown there as well. If the load is less than the maximum, consult a Michelin dealer for the correct inflation pressure for the specific load and add 10 psi. Michelin will supply a copy of the company's "Recreational Vehicle Tire Guide" on request by calling 1-(800) 847-3435.

Overloading

If a trip to the scales seems too much trouble, and the owner is prone to simply assume that inflating to the pressure listed on the tire sidewall is okay, hazards still exist because the tires may be overloaded (a common occurrence). Weighing a motorhome is a very important safety consideration *(see Chapter 1)*. Individual wheel scales often are unavailable, but it's possible to weigh a motorhome's axles individually on a platform scale.

TIPS THAT WORK

True Traction

Sometimes, a vehicle stuck in mud or sand only needs to move a few inches in order to regain traction. In such situations, I have successfully used two pieces of metal-mesh plasterer's lath to extract my vehicle. By placing the lath sections either in front of or behind the drive axle wheels (depending on the best escape route), both tires will grip and allow enough movement to get the vehicle back onto a solid footing. Not only will the lath help extract your vehicle from a frustrating, sometimes dangerous predicament, it also will save a great deal of wear and tear on your vehicle's driveline and tires. Of course, if a tow truck is not needed, you also will benefit financially.

The amount of lath material required is approximately 10×30 inches, depending primarily on tire size. The metal mesh is available at building-supply stores and is normally paint-primed or galvanized. It doesn't seem to rust, is easily stored flat just about anywhere aboard an RV, and can be used over and over. This method works on ice, snow, mud, and sand.

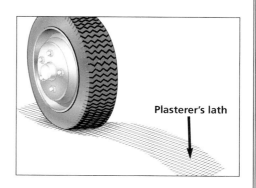

Plasterer's lath

Lloyd Schick, Surrey, British Columbia, Canada

Again, if the motorhome's tires are loaded to their maximums, 10 psi can be added to the inflation pressure shown on the tire sidewall. The extra pressure does not increase the load-carrying capacity of the tire.

A common situation in which the additional 10 psi may be desirable is when the vehicle tends to wander. Some vehicles wander more with tires that are inflated to the minimum pressure for the actual load than when higher pressures are used. Correction of a wander problem should start by weighing the vehicle. Begin with minimum inflation pressures for the actual load and adjust pressures upward in stages (not exceeding the cold-inflation pressure molded on the tire sidewall, plus 10 psi for light-truck tires) to determine the ideal pressure for minimum vehicle wander.

Tire inflation should be checked prior to each trip, at least once a week during trips, and a visual check should be made each morning. Always check pressures when tires are cold. A visual check of tires should be included in a routine walkaround inspection that occurs every time you take a break from driving. Tires build pressure while the vehicle is moving, and the pressure increase is taken into account in the manufacturer's (cold) inflation-pressure recommendation. Thus, if you begin the day with tires at 45 psi and find them at 50 psi later, don't reduce the pressure. When the temperature drops, the tires will return to the original 45 psi.

Finally, make sure your pressure gauge is accurate! Ask your tire dealer to verify it.

Figure 2.3: The result of heat caused by underinflation and/or over-loading is tire delamination and failure.

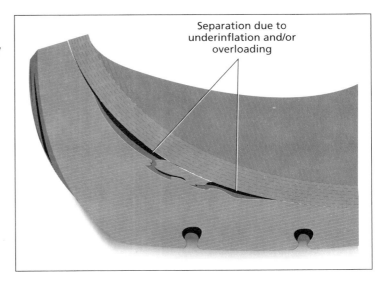

Separation due to underinflation and/or overloading

TIRE DAMAGE YOU CAN'T SEE

The significance of proper inflation and loading is not appreciated by most drivers because the results of underinflation and/or overloading often don't show up immediately. A temporarily underinflated/overloaded tire may fail long after the inadequacy has been corrected, depending on driving conditions.

Heat is a tire's worst enemy, and excessive heat is the result of underinflation/overloading, as well as the cause of tread separation *(Figure 2.3)*.

When the temperature of the tire's core compound exceeds approximately 250°F, cords lose strength; the bond is loosened between the cords and the surrounding rubber compound, making the tire more susceptible to failure. If the owner escapes a failure and is not even aware of the underinflation until later, the underinflation incident then appears to have had no consequence. To the contrary, an overheated tire does not cool to its original strength; it is permanently weakened, and a blowout or tread separation probably will occur later, after the underinflation incident is long forgotten. When the tire eventually fails, the owner may blame it on manufacturing defects or poor quality when in fact the tire was damaged by negligence.

When is a tire overheated? It's not practical to measure tire temperature with a thermometer, so the primary defenses against excessive heat are proper loading and adequate inflation. The worst condition is traveling superheated highways, so it's best to avoid the heat of the day in summer, if possible.

Damage from tire overloading and/or underinflation can be readily detected by tire service personnel. Such tires often rupture in the upper sidewall area after cords break. The evidence may be ripples, bulges, soft spots, wrinkles, creases, or other signs of weakness in the sidewall.

HOW TO MAKE TIRES LAST LONGER

In addition to proper inflation and loading, routine tire rotation is important to tire longevity. Even though we attempt to maintain ideal inflation pressures to maximize a tire's footprint, it may be impossible to avoid at least limited overinflation when loads vary. Accelerated tire wear may be inevitable with bias-ply, but proper tire rotation can hold it to a minimum. Radial tires are minimally affected by overinflation.

Again, tire companies differ. At least one major truck-tire manufacturer says it's not necessary to rotate unless abnormal wear is noticed but suggests consulting the vehicle owner's manual for a rotation recommendation. Others assert tires should be rotated before improper wear characteristics are visible. Chevrolet's motorhome chassis owners manual recommends rotation every 6,000 to 8,000 miles, emphasizing that the first rotation is the most important. If you notice abnormal wear, have the alignment checked and rotate tires immediately.

If abnormal tread wear becomes noticeable, some manufacturers say it's too late for maximum tire life because a pattern of uneven wear, once established, may be impossible to reverse.

The cost of rotating tires varies with the type of vehicle and can be somewhat expensive for motorhomes. Owners who are reluctant to rotate tires regularly should inspect them closely, and measure tread depths with a gauge (available in auto-supply stores).

SOME CAUSES OF IMPROPER TIRE WEAR

Some causes of improper tire wear may be apparent, while others are more difficult to diagnose.

- **Irregular wear** (Also called heel/toe wear) Tread blocks wear more on one end (longitudinally) than the other. This wear pattern may indicate worn suspension parts, but in many flotation and mud/snow treads it's a characteristic of the tire design. Rotate frequently to keep adverse wear patterns from becoming severe.

- **Improper camber** One shoulder of front tire will wear more quickly than the other.

- **Excessive toe-in/toe-out** Rapid, uneven wear on front tires, often feathering the edges of tread serrations.

- **Overinflation** Center of tread will wear more quickly than shoulders (primarily with bias-ply tires).

- **Underinflation** Shoulders will wear faster than center of tread, and tread may tend to ripple.

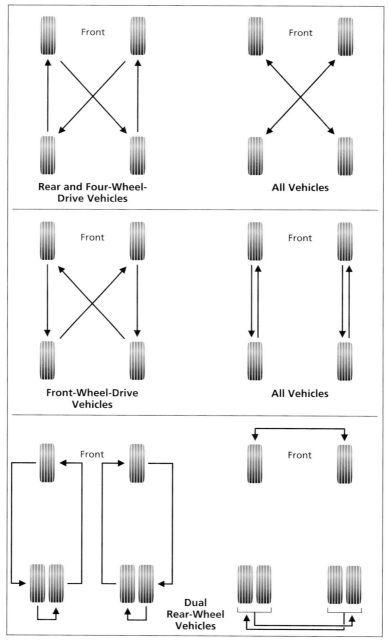

Figure 2.4: Best possible wear depends substantially on regular tire rotation, particularly when abnormal wear patterns are evident. Tires need not remain in their original direction of rotation.

When rotation is deemed necessary, use the pattern recommended by the manufacturer of your vehicle, or use one of the patterns featured in Figure 2.4. The original rolling direction of tires does not need to be maintained unless tread design dictates a specific direction! The rolling direction can be reversed by moving the tire to the opposite side of the vehicle (as indicated), except when using mud/snow tires that are clearly designed for best traction in a specific rolling direction.

Use of Blocks

Also important to tire life is proper use of blocks while leveling. The entire footprint of the tire should be supported by blocks, with no tread hanging over the sides, which exerts excessive stress on the tire cords *(Figure 2.5)*.

Summarizing, the keys to extended tire life are:

- Proper inflation for the specific load
- Proper loading
- Proper tire rotation
- Proper wheel alignment and use of effective shock absorbers.

TIPS THAT WORK

Tire Cover Saver

To protect our RV tires from weathering and sun rot, I purchased vinyl tire covers. In the high winds of Texas and the coastal areas, the covers would blow off the wheels. As a solution to the problem, I purchased elastic cord and metal S-chain-end links from the hardware store. (Elastic cord can also be found at boat and canvas dealers.) I measured the diameter of the wheel, and doubled this figure for the cord length. I found that a 56-inch length was just right for our 15-inch tires. I tied an S-link onto each end of the cord, and slipped it over the rear of the tire and cover. The ends are brought around to the front and the elastic cord ends are hooked together. Now the tire covers stay put, even in strong winds.

Carl R. Hartup,
Fort Wayne, IN

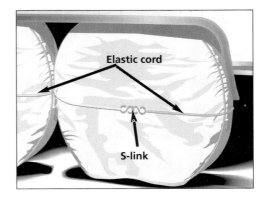

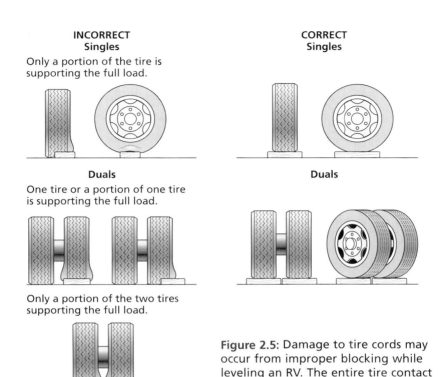

INCORRECT
Singles
Only a portion of the tire is
supporting the full load.

CORRECT
Singles

Duals
One tire or a portion of one tire
is supporting the full load.

Duals

Only a portion of the two tires
supporting the full load.

Figure 2.5: Damage to tire cords may occur from improper blocking while leveling an RV. The entire tire contact surface must be supported.

Tire Composition

Tires vary widely in design as well as materials. We usually think of tires as made of rubber, but in fact natural rubber is a relatively minor ingredient. The basic building blocks of the rubber compound are polymers, combinations of natural rubber and two types of synthetic rubber. These combinations vary with the intended use. Another important building block is carbon black, a reinforcing material that provides strength in the rubber compounds. Actually glorified soot, its use in conjunction with rubber provides the matrix structure that gives strength. Then there are oils, used as softeners to provide traction within the compound. A high-performance tire will have more oils, helping the tire conform to the road.

Next, sulfur is used as a cross-linking agent or network to keep the carbon black and rubber together for strength and flexibility.

Accelerators control the rate of cure of the rubber compound. Finally, antioxidants and antiozodants are used for protection.

Radial-ply tires dominate the market today with a few bias-ply tires still available for trailers. The radials are available with steel belts or a combination of fabric and steel. Tires with all-steel belts are preferred in the trucking industry for their performance as well as retreadability.

TIPS THAT WORK

Maintenance Anxiety

After pulling a fifth-wheel trailer for several years, and trying to keep track of its accumulated mileage for service purposes, I struck upon the idea of installing a hub odometer like the truckers use. I checked with a truck-parts store, and found they needed specific information prior to special-ordering such a product for me.

Because a hub odometer records mileage based on wheel revolutions, it is first necessary to determine tire circumference of the vehicle to be equipped. My rig has LT 245/75R-16 tires with 93-inch circumferences. After discerning this figure, I multiplied the number of feet in a statute mile (5,280) by 12. This told me that there are 63,360 inches per mile. I divided this number by 93 inches to arrive at 681.3 tire revolutions per mile.

Then I ordered an Accu-Trak hub odometer (model no. AT-31), which is designed for 680 tire revolutions per mile, from a truck-equipment dealer. I can now check the hub odometer to find the actual accumulated trailer mileage. This tells me when I need to have the brakes adjusted, the wheel bearings repacked, and the tires rotated.

It is a simple and inexpensive job to install a hub odometer. The model I purchased came with a mounting bracket that fits over two wheel studs; cost was $38.90. Also, as was the case with my fifth-wheel, the odometer can be used with wheel covers by drilling a hole in the center of the cover. I think every new trailer should come with a hub odometer already installed.

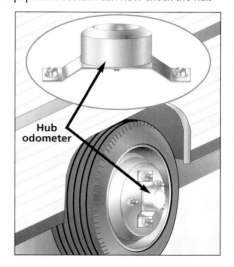

Hub odometer

Melvin Perkins
Missoula, MT

CHOOSING REPLACEMENT TIRES

When choosing replacement tires for a vehicle, the replacements can usually duplicate the original tire size and type if the original tires have provided good service. Exceptions include overload situations.

If a tire has worn abnormally fast, with accelerated wear on the shoulders of the tread, the tire probably has been overloaded and/or underinflated. The vehicle should be weighed (loaded) before purchasing new tires to make sure the tire-load capacity is adequate. Don't rely on the vehicle's load ratings for tire selection because an overloaded vehicle may exceed the load ratings of either or both axles. Weighing the vehicle by axle or, preferably, by each wheel is very important when abnormal tire wear suggests overloading has occurred.

If failures have occurred and a trip to the scales indicates an overload, selection of tires with higher load ratings may be appropriate. However, be aware that tire overloading usually is a reliable indicator that other chassis components are overloaded as well and that weight is beyond the unit's GVWR. Use of higher-rated tires will not prevent accelerated wear and/or failure of other components, including wheels. The load and inflation pressure ratings of larger tires may exceed the load and inflation pressure ratings of the wheels. Check with a tire dealer regarding tire/wheel load and inflation pressure matching.

Unfortunately there are few reliable ways to compare truck-, light-truck, and trailer-tire quality other than by the manufacturer's reputation, although speed and wear parameters are available for passenger-car tires. Tires that look the same are not necessarily the same because the quality of the materials—particularly the rubber compound—can vary widely. Poor-quality tires shed tread material rapidly, while those of good quality have high resistance to tread wear. All-purpose and mud/snow tires generally wear faster than tires with highway tread. Tire compounding is a compromise aimed at providing the optimum mixture of performance characteristics for the intended use.

Passenger Tire Designations

Passenger tires display government-mandated grades for quality and speed. The speed-rating system uses letters, commonly S (112 MPH) and V (above 130 MPH) in combination with load index numbers that indicate the capacity of the tire. Example: reference numbers 97S following the size designation mean the tire's maximum load is 1,609 pounds and its speed rating is 112 MPH. The tire also will carry specific maximum load and inflation ratings.

Treadwear ratings vary from 60 to 500, with higher numbers indicating higher tread durability. Traction grades range from A to C, with A being the highest grade available. Temperature grades range from A to C, again with A being highest, indicating a tire's ability to dissipate heat.

Trailer Tires

When choosing trailer tires, any of three types (car, light truck, or special trailer) can be used, providing the load range is adequate for the weight, and the wheels are suitable. Special Trailer (ST) tires are compounded for extra resistance to deterioration (cracking) from the effects of the sun and ozone in the air and are preferred because most RV owners take several years to wear out a set of tires. In addition, trailer tires usually fit into the Extra Load category, which is identified on the tire sidewall.

When using passenger tires on trailers, the Tire and Rim Association recommends reducing their load ratings by 9 percent. The reason is not that trailers inherently are harder on tires, but that they are capable of being overloaded more dramatically than are passenger cars.

Radials on Trailers

Most trailers are fitted with radial tires at the factory. When replacing them, choose the same size and load rating unless abnormal tire wear or failures have occurred.

When choosing replacement tires, select load capacity high enough to insure that the tires are not loaded to their maximums. If your trailer load requires tires with considerably higher ratings than were originally fitted, and those tires require higher inflation pressures, new wheels with higher load and inflation-pressure ratings may be necessary. Check existing wheels for inflation-pressure maximum ratings and for load maximums.

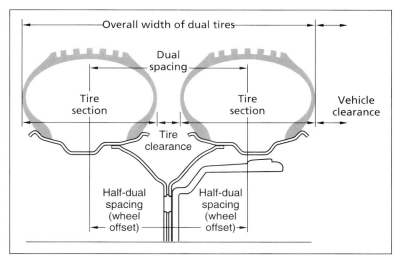

Figure 2.6: Proper spacing of dual tires is important to prevent sidewall contact, which can result in damage.

Dual-Tire Spacing

When choosing tires that are a different size from the originals for a motorhome or truck with dual rear tires, pay close attention to wheel size and to spacing of the rear tires. Dual-wheel spacing is measured from the center line of one tire to the center line of the other *(Figure 2.6)*. Insufficient dual spacing causes the insides of the tire sidewalls to touch, which results in excessive heat and sidewall wear. In addition, rocks or debris can be trapped more easily between the tires, causing punctures. Tire chains cannot be used when dual spacing is inadequate.

Tire and Wheel Matching

Tires used as sets on a dual-wheel axle must be properly matched. The tires should have the same size designation, be of the same type, and have the same or nearly the same outside diameters. Mismatched dual sets cause friction and heat because one tire is larger than the other, which causes slippage, excessive heat, and wear in both tires. Tire diameter should not vary more than ¼ inch (tires inflated equally). Diameter can be calculated by measuring circumference with a steel tape measure that conforms properly to the tire or by marking

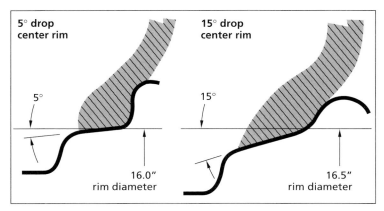

5° drop center rim

15° drop center rim

5°

15°

16.0"
rim diameter

16.5"
rim diameter

Figure 2.7: Rim contours differ for varying tire designs. Incorrect tire/rim combinations create danger.

the tire and ground with chalk, driving forward, and measuring the distance between chalk marks. Divide the circumference measurement by 3.1416 to get diameter. If tires are new, wait at least twenty-four hours after initial inflation to check diameters.

When replacement tires exceed the load rating of the original tires, wheel suitability becomes an important factor. For example, original motorhome 8R19.5 load-range D tires may be due for replacement, and the owner may assume that moving up to the E-load range would offer an extra margin of safety. Unfortunately, the reverse may be true with many chassis, such as Chevrolet. The original wheels supplied with the gasoline-powered chassis having the highest GVWR were rated for 2,780 pounds maximum load and 95 psi maximum inflation pressure, suitable for 8R19.5 tires rated for 2,800 pounds at 80 psi in load range-D. When moving up to load-range E, the tire is rated for 3,170 pounds at 95 psi; in load-range F the tire is rated for 3,500 pounds at 110 psi.

The load as well as inflation limits of the 8R19.5 load-range E or F tires are beyond the load-carrying capacity of the wheel. Load-range E or F tires should not be used on wheels designed for maximum load/inflation of load-range D tires because their sidewall markings will encourage wheel overloading and overinflation.

Tire Mixing

If radial and bias-ply tires must be mixed, the radials should be used on the rear to prevent oversteer.

When changing tire sizes, more than one rim width usually is specified as suitable. For example, rim widths of 5½ to 7 inches may be specified for a 15-inch tire. The wider rims offer better road stability, but are more easily damaged when striking curbs or other obstacles.

Make sure replacement tires are of the correct size and contour for the rims.

Warning: It's possible to fit a 16-inch tire on a 16½-inch rim, but the tire cannot be safely inflated or used. In addition to the size error, rim contours are not correct. The 16-inch tire requires a 5-degree drop-center rim while the 16½-inch tire requires a 15-degree drop-center rim *(Figure 2.7)*.

Calculating Effect on Performance

When purchasing replacement tires of a different size from the originals, it's wise to estimate the effect on performance. Tires that are larger in diameter than the originals will have the effect of lowering the numerical axle ratio. The opposite is true of smaller-than-original tires. A formula can be used to calculate the difference (rpm is revolutions per mile):

$$\frac{\text{Original Tire rpm}}{\text{New Tire rpm}} \times \frac{\text{Indicated}}{\text{Speed}} = \frac{\text{Actual}}{\text{Speed}}$$

The actual axle ratio does not change, but the relationship between engine rpm and road speed is altered as if the axle ratio had been changed. The reason is that the larger replacement tires will travel farther in one revolution than will the original tires. The reverse is true for smaller tires. Speedometer error caused by a change in tire size also can be calculated:

$$\frac{\text{New Tire rpm}}{\text{Original Tire rpm}} \times \frac{\text{Original}}{\text{Axle Ratio}} = \frac{\text{Effective}}{\text{Axle Ratio}}$$

Tire rpm can be calculated from measurement of circumference. Measure the tire's circumference with a steel tape measure. Divide the circumference (inches) into 63,360 (the number of inches in a mile), and the result is approximate revolutions per mile.

A speedometer shop can recalibrate if the error created by a tire change is excessive—more than 3 or 4 MPH.

Aging and Ozone Cracking

RVs normally are not driven as far each year as family or business vehicles. Thus tires last longer and are more subject to deterioration from ozone in the air and the effects of sunlight. Protectants blended into the tire compound gradually bleed to the surface of the tire to provide some protection when the vehicle is used regularly. When it is parked for long periods, as is typical of RVs, the protectants do not bleed to the surface as rapidly, and the tire is more susceptible to damage.

Surface cracks usually are not a problem. But when the cracks extend into the tire compound, durability is affected. According to Michelin North America, cracks that are $1/32$ inch deep should not cause concern. Between $1/32$ inch and $1/16$ inch, the tire is suspect and should be examined by a tire dealer. If cracks are deeper than $1/16$ inch the tire should be replaced.

Cracking can be retarded by excercising proper care:

- Cover the tires when the vehicle is in storage, even for a few days
- Keep tires clean
- Keep tires properly inflated
- Do not park the vehicle near electric generators or transformers, where welding is in progress, or inside a building equipped with mercury vapor lamps
- Do not use tire dressings and other products that contain petroleum distillates or alcohol

Time for Replacement

The Rubber Manufacturers Association recommends that tires on vehicles of more than 10,000 pounds gross weight be replaced when less than $1/8$ inch of tread depth remains (not including tread-wear indicators). On vehicles less than 10,000 pounds gross weight, front tires should be replaced when worn to tread-wear indicators, or when $1/16$ inch or less of tread remains. At least one major tire company recommends that tires be replaced if they are more than seven years old, regardless of the amount of tread remaining.

A tire's age can be determined by the DOT number molded on the sidewall. The last digit on the right represents the last digit of the year of production. The decade (1990s) is indicated by a triangle to the right of the last digit.

ABOUT WHEELS

A wheel is composed of a rim and a disc. The tire is mounted on the rim and the disc is used to attach the wheel to the vehicle. The assembly will vary widely in design, depending on tire size, type, and vehicle application. Wheels are tested by their manufacturers to withstand specific maximum weights and air pressures. All wheels are rated for maximum load and inflation pressures, although the ratings are not always marked on the wheels. It may be necessary to check with the wheel manufacturer.

Errors are common in wheel selection when replacement tires are purchased, and errors are common even at the RV-factory level, especially when styled wheels are used. Many styled wheels are rated for less than 2,000 pounds. Few tire dealers pay much attention to the fact that the wheel has limits and that the tires and wheels must be compatible. It is dangerous to mount a tire rated, for example, at 3,000 pounds on a wheel rated at 2,000, although it happens often. Few wheels break, but when they do, it is with explosive force, possibly resulting in an accident.

Determining Suitability for Radials

A decision to replace bias-ply tires with radials on an older vehicle, especially a motorhome, should be preceded by an inspection of the wheels for the word radial or by a circled R stamped on the rims that will indicate suitability for use of radial tires. If the wheel does not have these markings, it may not be designed for radials, and the wheel manufacturer should be consulted regarding the wheel's rating. Few trailer wheels have these markings, although many are suitable for radials.

Wheels used on trailers may be passenger-car type, light-truck type, or they may be specifically designed for use on trailers. Late-model wheels usually are suitable for use with radial tires. Wheels on earlier trailers probably weren't specifically designed for radials, but are not typically prone to break unless tires are loaded to their maximums. When in doubt about wheel suitability, contact the wheel manufacturer for information on radial-tire use and for load and inflation-pressure ratings.

Figure 2.8: When changing wheels, measurement of offset will indicate if the new wheel has proper clearance from suspension and body components.

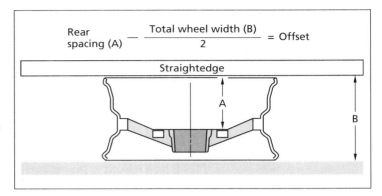

$$\text{Rear spacing (A)} - \frac{\text{Total wheel width (B)}}{2} = \text{Offset}$$

Figure 2.9: Offset can be calculated even if the tire is mounted on the wheel.

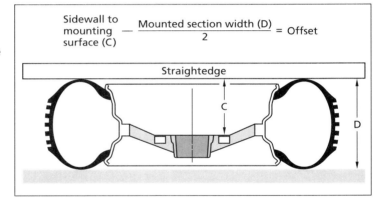

$$\text{Sidewall to mounting surface (C)} - \frac{\text{Mounted section width (D)}}{2} = \text{Offset}$$

Wheel Dimensions

Styled replacement wheels have become very popular during the last decade, and it's helpful to know how to check dimensions before choosing replacement wheels.

When buying new wheels, make sure they are approved for the tires that will be used. Your tire dealer has additional listings. It's wise to measure wheel offset when comparing new wheels with the originals.

Offset is the difference in distance between the center line of the rim and the mounting surface (surface of the bolt pad that contacts the hub). A wheel with negative offset positions the tire farther from the vehicle's frame, widening the vehicle's track. Positive offset moves the tire inward, reducing the vehicle's track. When offset is zero, the disc is positioned in the center of the rim.

To calculate offset it's necessary to measure wheel spacing. Divide the total wheel width (B) by 2 and subtract the result from rear spacing (A) to get offset in positive or negative *(Figure 2.8)*. Use the same formula to calculate offset with a tire mounted on the wheel *(Figure 2.9)*. Divide section width (D) by 2 and subtract that figure from rear spacing (C) to get offset. Figures for the wheel alone and for the wheel with a tire mounted on it are valid for comparison.

TIRE STORAGE

When the vehicle is out of service, cover all tires and maintain correct inflation pressure. It is not necessary to elevate the vehicle.

Tires are a critically valuable component of any vehicle. When proper care is taken, they should provide the performance and safety of which they're capable.

Selecting a Tow Vehicle

In this chapter the following items will be covered:

- Selecting Your Vehicle Type
- New Tow Vehicles
- Axle Ratios
- Choosing an Engine
- Optional Towing Equipment
- Auxiliary Oil Cooling
- Used Tow Vehicles

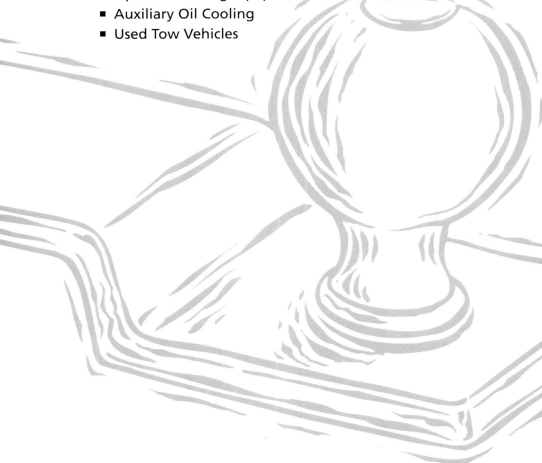

*H*omework is the key to selecting a tow vehicle that will per
form and handle properly with the trailer of your choice.
Homework is necessary because, in most cases, salesmen will
pressure prospective buyers to take whatever is on the sales lot at the
time, whether or not it is properly equipped. All too often, the salesman has not read the manufacturer's towing brochure. Thus it's fully
up to the buyer to make the right choice.

Most motor-vehicle manufacturers offer a considerable amount of
specific information on vehicle types and how they should be
equipped in the form of trailer-towing guides. However, selecting a
suitable used tow vehicle involves some additional guesswork. It's not
always possible to find a used vehicle equipped with specialized towing options, even if the buyer knows which towing options were available when the vehicle was new.

Trailer Life's Towing Guide contains ratings designed to solve that
problem—ratings for passenger cars, light trucks, vans, and sport-utility vehicles, beginning with the most recent model year and dating
back five years. The Towing Guide, combined with the information
provided in this chapter, offers you the ability to make an intelligent,
accurate tow-vehicle choice.

SELECTING YOUR VEHICLE TYPE

Consider the following points when choosing between a car, truck,
sport-utility vehicle, or van for towing:

- Evaluate your needs and desires. How many people will accompany you? Where do you like to drive? Regardless of what might
  work best, do you prefer a passenger car, truck, or van? If you
  prefer a car, is your trailer too large and heavy to be towed by the
  model that interests you?

- Make sure the vehicle's overall size and wheelbase are adequate
  for the trailer in question. Check *Trailer Life's Towing Guide.*
  Evaluate the drivetrain in view of the ratings. Engine performance
  and axle ratio, which are critical elements in determining if the
  vehicle will adequately tow your trailer, must be appropriate to
  handle the weight of your trailer.

- Tires should have adequate capacity for the weight of passengers and supplies in the vehicle, as well as for that portion of hitch weight carried by the tow vehicle. (A load-distributing hitch distributes hitch weight to all axles of the tow vehicle and trailer, with the tow vehicle carrying about two-thirds of the hitch weight and the remainder transferred to the trailer wheels.)
- Suspension components should also be adequate for the load. The vehicle should have a heavy-duty radiator, which usually is standard if the vehicle has factory air conditioning. If a new vehicle is being purchased, the manufacturer's trailer-towing package, which includes special heavy-duty cooling options, should be ordered.
- Evaluate the mechanical condition of the vehicle if it is not new.

NEW TOW VEHICLES

Covering all the bases in selecting a new tow vehicle may sound like quite a project. And it would be without the benefit of manufacturers' trailer-towing brochures *(Figure 3.1)*. A purchase should not be made before you read the appropriate brochures for the vehicles you are considering.

All domestic manufacturers and most foreign companies offer towing guides in one form or another. Some guides are abbreviated, while others are extensive and educational, even beyond simply listing specifications for the brand in question.

The most comprehensive guides are published by Ford and Chevrolet, which also have developed the most extensive option packages for towing. Chrysler Corporation does a good job in trucks and vans, but does little with passenger cars. Among Japanese manufacturers, Toyota, Nissan, and Mazda offer trucks with ratings up to 5,900 pounds, and a variety of Japanese SUVs will tow trailers up to 5,000 pounds. Most Japanese cars are rated for maximums of 1,000 pounds, if they're rated at all. In the absence of a towing brochure, check the vehicle-owner's manual.

Most midsize or larger cars will tow 2,000 to 3,000 pounds without special options, and their manufacturers offer special packages for towing more than 2,000 pounds. More specific options are required or recommended for trailer weights above 3,500 pounds, which is the

Figure 3.1: Manufacturers' towing guides offer detailed advice on equipment selection and trailer weight limits.

weight level separating the companies that are serious about towing from the companies that don't give it much consideration.

When you visit a dealership, you should already know what the manufacturer recommends for the weight of your trailer with full water and propane tanks and all your supplies aboard. That weight can be calculated by adding the amount of weight you anticipate taking on trips to the UVW (unloaded vehicle weight) listing for your trailer. If your trailer is a pre-1997 model and does not have the RVIA weight label introduced during that year, which lists the UVW, note the dry weight of the unit and calculate the amount of weight you will add.

To estimate the weight of what you will add:

Water	8.2 pounds per gallon
Propane	4.25 pounds per gallon

If your trailer's sticker does not include a UVW number, add the weight of one or two batteries because, prior to the change in weight-listings format during 1997, trailer manufacturers generally did not include them in their dry-weight figures. (Batteries weigh 50 to 60 pounds each.) If you already own the trailer, take it to a commercial scale *(see Chapter 1)*.

While examining vehicle manufacturers' literature, take particular note of two recommended weight limits:

1. Maximum gross trailer weight
2. Maximum gross combination weight

Maximum gross trailer weight is the maximum weight of the trailer and all its contents. Maximum gross combination weight is the maximum weight of the trailer as well as the tow vehicle and all their contents. This includes fuel, water, supplies, and passengers.

In order to calculate the actual gross combination weight of a tow vehicle and trailer, actual weight of the tow vehicle must be determined. With a new tow vehicle, ask the dealer to check his reference books for the base curb weight, which is the weight of the vehicle with a full tank of fuel and standard equipment. The dealer also can supply listings for weight of specific options, which are important to add because their weight can be substantial, especially in the case of an optional diesel engine.

With reasonably accurate weight figures in hand, choose a tow vehicle that is rated to handle about 10 percent more than the calculated weight, as a margin of safety. RV owners hardly ever underestimate the weight of their vehicles.

The ratings are the keys to safe towing and adequate performance, and they also have a bearing on fuel economy. *(See also Chapter 1, Weight Handling and Safety and Chapter 4, Towing Safety.)*

If you're buying a new or used travel trailer, pay particular attention to the proportion between hitch weight and gross weight because this denotes the trailer's balance and is the key to how well it handles. If hitch weight is insufficient, this often means mediocre or poor handling. If you already own a trailer with minimum hitch weight (10 percent of gross weight or less), or have found one like that with a floor plan you simply can't resist, you'll need to select a tow vehicle that has as much inherent stability as possible. That means a truck or van with maximum wheelbase length and minimum rear overhang.

With a good understanding of the weight situation, you're ready to shop for the proper tow vehicle. The trailer-towing brochures will offer detailed information. The highest trailer-weight rating for new passenger cars is 5,000 pounds. Chevrolet and Cadillac large rear-wheel-drive cars were discontinued in 1996, taking with them 5,000-pound (Chevrolet) and 7,000-pound (Cadillac) trailer-weight ratings. Ford's Crown Victoria, previously rated at 5,000 pounds, was dropped to 2,000 pounds. But, the Lincoln Town Car continued with a 5,000-pound tow rating for the 1997 model year.

Trucks, sport-utility vehicles, and vans are more suitable than cars as tow vehicles for trailers that weigh more than 5,000 pounds (loaded weight) because of their larger engines, numerically higher axle ratios (higher numbers mean better pulling power), improved engine cooling, heavier suspensions, and longer wheelbases (in some cases). However, a passenger car can do the job nicely if weight is not excessive, the trailer is well balanced (being aerodynamic also helps), and driving conditions are not too severe.

AXLE RATIOS

The choice of engine size versus axle ratio often is difficult for the tow-vehicle buyer. The axle ratio is the relationship between drive-shaft revolutions and wheel revolutions (*see Figure 3.2*). For example, in a vehicle with a 3.50:1 axle ratio, the driveshaft revolves 3.5 times for each revolution of the wheels. As you can see, more driveshaft revolutions for each wheel revolution mean more torque multiplication. Ideal axle ratios for driving without the trailer are numerically high, such as 3.08:1. They keep engine rpm at minimum levels for best possible fuel economy. But they are not well suited to moving large amounts of weight. Typical axle ratios for passenger cars range from 3.00:1 to 3.42:1, while typical ratios for light trucks range from 3.25:1 to 4.56:1.

The choice of axle ratio for a tow vehicle is a compromise between fuel economy in solo driving and performance while towing. Numerically high ratios are better for power and worse for mileage,

Figure 3.2:
Selecting the
proper axle
ratio is impor-
tant to per-
formance and
fuel economy.
The ratio
indicates
the proportion
between
the pinion shaft
and axle shaft
revolutions.

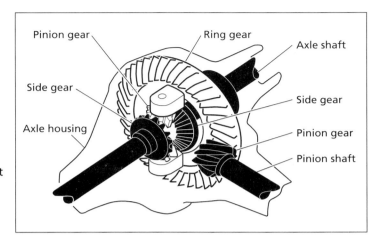

and numerically low ratios are just the opposite. Fortunately, four-speed-automatic and five-speed-manual transmissions in cars and light trucks have reduced the penalty of this compromise. Their over-drive top gears give the vehicle a "tall" solo cruising-gear ratio even if a "torquey" axle ratio such as 3.73:1 or 4.10:1 is chosen in the interest of good towing performance in mountainous terrain.

CHOOSING AN ENGINE

Engine selection may seem confusing because more than one may be suitable for your trailer weight. The manufacturer's towing ratings are designed for typical driving conditions, which assume medium to low altitude. An engine loses about 3 percent of its horsepower for each 1,000 feet of rise in elevation. Thus, at 10,000 feet elevation, about 30 percent of the available horsepower has been lost *(Figure 3.3)*. When a considerable amount of travel at high altitudes is planned, the vehicle's towing rating should be reduced by about 2 percent per 1,000 feet in elevation above sea level.

Typically, buyers are torn between the smaller engines for fuel economy and the larger engines for performance. When trailer weight is in the middle to upper middle of the weight-rating category for a given engine/vehicle combination, the mid-size engine is valid for good performance. When trailer weight approaches the maximum, the pros-pective buyer must examine his or her travel habits and priorities very closely.

For example, a trailerist has a 32-foot fifth-wheel trailer that weighs 8,000 pounds, loaded for a trip. He is considering a Chevrolet C2500, either with the Vortec 5700 (5.7 liters) or 7400 (7.4 liters) gasoline engines, and is having trouble deciding between the two. The differences: The 5700 should get better fuel economy during solo driving but have substantially less muscle for climbing grades than the 7400. However, the 5700 is a very willing performer. The decision should favor the 5700 if most towing is in low elevations, and the buyer is not heavily performance oriented. The 7400 is preferred if considerable mountain travel is planned and/or if the buyer wants to maintain a relatively fast pace. One buyer's definition of "adequate" performance may be quite different from that of another, so personal preferences are important factors.

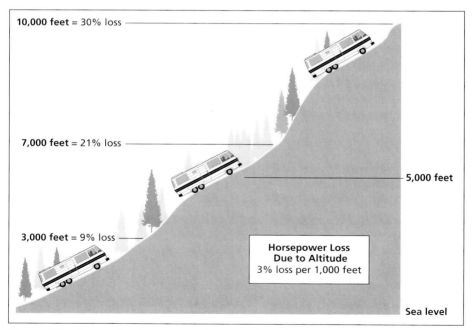

10,000 feet = 30% loss

7,000 feet = 21% loss

5,000 feet

3,000 feet = 9% loss

**Horsepower Loss
Due to Altitude**
3% loss per 1,000 feet

Sea level

Figure 3.3.: Atmospheric pressure drops as altitude increases, reducing performance of naturally aspirated engines.

OPTIONAL TOWING EQUIPMENT

Manufacturers of tow vehicles that receive serious attention by trailerists offer special trailer-towing-equipment packages, which usually are good values. The packages may range from very simple, possibly including only a wiring harness and a few other minor items, to a large package priced at several hundred dollars that includes a hitch receiver.

The prospective buyer should order the towing package and closely analyze the option list for other items that might be ordered, some of which are essential to towing performance and others that are merely for convenience and comfort. For heavy towing the list should include:

- Heavy-duty radiator
- Heavy-duty transmission-oil cooling
- Engine-oil cooler (for the higher weight categories)
- Hitch receiver
- Heavy-duty shock absorbers
- Front stabilizer bar
- High-output alternator
- High-capacity battery
- Cruise control
- Increased fuel capacity
- Positive-traction differential
- Trailering wiring harness
- Extended mirrors

External engine-oil cooling is available only on a few large V-8s in trucks and vans and is a worthwhile option if offered. Some companies offer factory-installed auxiliary transmission-oil coolers, while others increase the size of the transmission-oil cooling tank inside the radiator. In the latter situation, it's often wise to add an auxiliary transmission-oil cooler if the vehicle will be used for heavy towing in mountainous terrain.

The hitch receiver usually is an aftermarket item but also can be ordered from the factory. In fact, trailer-towing packages usually include the hitch receiver. It's wise to order heavy-duty springs in passenger cars and half-ton trucks and vans. In ¾- and 1-ton vans and trucks, ordering heavy-duty springs usually results in an excessively stiff ride, although some of the motor companies specify heavy-duty springs in their towing packages, especially for fifth-wheel towing. The only situation in which heavy-duty springs are needed in a ¾- or 1-ton van or truck is when hauling substantial amounts of weight in the vehicle in addition to towing a trailer. The problem with ordering excessively stiff springs is that the owner is stuck with the stiff ride. If, having ordered slightly lower-rated springs, the owner determines that additional suspension help is needed, air bags can be added.

Data books supplied to dealers can help you select the proper gross vehicle weight rating (GVWR), which dictates spring ratings, depending on your specific anticipated loading of the vehicle.

A high-capacity alternator is important only if your trailer is equipped with a refrigerator that is operated on 12-volt DC power while traveling. Otherwise, the standard alternator will suffice. Cruise control theoretically is a convenience item, albeit one that most of us feel we cannot do without. Increased fuel capacity is essential because of the adverse effect of towing on fuel consumption. A positive-traction differential is not necessary for towing but is generally helpful if the vehicle is to be driven often on slippery surfaces. Extended mirrors can be added later, but the ones that come from the factory may be of higher quality and usually are mounted more securely.

AUXILIARY OIL COOLING

Unless your trailer is light (below 3,000 pounds), and you know the vehicle is equipped with the optional factory-installed auxiliary or high-capacity transmission-oil cooling, it's usually wise to add an auxiliary transmission-oil cooler, available at any RV supply store.

If the vehicle is equipped only with warning lights to monitor engine functions, you'll need to add a gauge for coolant temperature. You might consider adding a multi-function gauge that monitors a variety of engine functions, including coolant, engine, and transmission-oil temperatures. Such gauges are available in the auto sections of some department stores and from automotive specialty stores.

USED TOW VEHICLES

   The manufacturer's recommendations serve as the primary guide in choosing vehicle type and drivetrain equipment for new vehicles. If you're in the market for a used vehicle, check the manufacturer's ratings provided in *Trailer Life's Towing Guide* to give you an idea of the engine sizes and axle ratios suitable for various trailer weights, along with the types of special equipment recommended or required by the manufacturer, and check the vehicles you're considering for similar equipment. Using the engine/axle ratio recommendations as guide-

USED-VEHICLE EVALUATION CHECKLIST

A thorough evaluation of any used vehicle should cover the following items:

❑ **Engine Condition** Cylinder compression is very important. Compression should not vary more than 10 percent from one cylinder to another. Check spark-plug condition (look for evidence of oil consumption). Black, wet-looking soot on spark plugs indicates that the engine uses excessive oil. If possible, have a qualified shop perform a cylinder-leak-down test, which will give an even better indication of the condition of piston rings and valves.

❑ **Cooling-system Condition** If the vehicle is not equipped with factory air conditioning, it probably does not have a heavy-duty radiator. Such a vehicle is more liable to overheat when used for towing, particularly if the trailer weighs more than 3,000 pounds. Beyond the size of the radiator, the condition of the cooling system is crucial. If the system has not been maintained, not only may the radiator be partially blocked by corrosion, but flow of coolant through the engine block may be restricted as well. A thorough check of the cooling system should be performed by a mechanic, including inspection of the radiator tubes for partial blockage.

❑ **Transmission** While driving the vehicle, pay close attention to shifting characteristics. The transmission should shift smoothly and without delay. It should downshift automatically when the accelerator pedal is pressed to the floor. Remove the dipstick and check the color and odor of the transmission fluid. (New fluid is red and has clarity.) If the transmission has been overheated, the oil will be darker than new fluid and will appear cloudy. It may also have an odor that is distinctively different than new fluid. Overheating causes transmission fluid to oxidize and lose lubricating ability.

lines, while not a guarantee of satisfaction, will usually get you closer to a proper choice than mere guesswork.

If the vehicle is being purchased from a private owner who has used it for towing, the owner's assessment of its performance may be helpful, although it should be taken with a grain of salt, since an optimistic description of the vehicle's towing prowess may help make the sale.

A thorough mechanical evaluation of a used vehicle by a reliable mechanic can also be helpful, if the vehicle's current owner will permit it.

Whether your choice of tow vehicle is new or used, the time you spend on research can pay off in good performance and trouble-free towing.

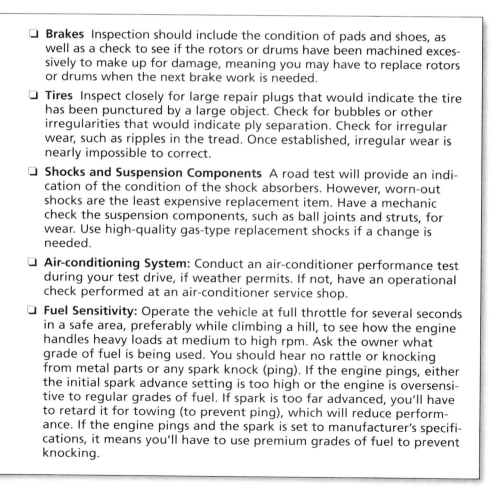

❑ **Brakes** Inspection should include the condition of pads and shoes, as well as a check to see if the rotors or drums have been machined excessively to make up for damage, meaning you may have to replace rotors or drums when the next brake work is needed.

❑ **Tires** Inspect closely for large repair plugs that would indicate the tire has been punctured by a large object. Check for bubbles or other irregularities that would indicate ply separation. Check for irregular wear, such as ripples in the tread. Once established, irregular wear is nearly impossible to correct.

❑ **Shocks and Suspension Components** A road test will provide an indication of the condition of the shock absorbers. However, worn-out shocks are the least expensive replacement item. Have a mechanic check the suspension components, such as ball joints and struts, for wear. Use high-quality gas-type replacement shocks if a change is needed.

❑ **Air-conditioning System:** Conduct an air-conditioner performance test during your test drive, if weather permits. If not, have an operational check performed at an air-conditioner service shop.

❑ **Fuel Sensitivity:** Operate the vehicle at full throttle for several seconds in a safe area, preferably while climbing a hill, to see how the engine handles heavy loads at medium to high rpm. Ask the owner what grade of fuel is being used. You should hear no rattle or knocking from metal parts or any spark knock (ping). If the engine pings, either the initial spark advance setting is too high or the engine is oversensitive to regular grades of fuel. If spark is too far advanced, you'll have to retard it for towing (to prevent ping), which will reduce performance. If the engine pings and the spark is set to manufacturer's specifications, it means you'll have to use premium grades of fuel to prevent knocking.

Towing Safety

In this chapter the following items will be covered:

- Weight and Balance
- Stability Checkup
- How a Trailer Should Handle
- Evaluating the Trailer and Hitch
- Proper Hitch Adjustment
- Corrective DrivingTechniques
- Equipment Maintenance

Although the basics of towing a trailer with a motor vehicle may seem rather simple—we've all towed rental trailers at one time or another—the dynamics of trailering can get rather complex. Indeed, the important criteria escape most trailerists, who may endure poor towing characteristics for many years without knowing the reason or realizing that something can be done about it.

Here, we'll go through a step-by-step procedure for evaluating tow-vehicle/trailer stability, followed by procedures for improving handling.

Trailers as well as tow vehicles have certain drawbacks: Trailers vary widely in weight distribution, while tow vehicles can vary widely in basic roadworthiness. Being confronted by one of these situations is unfortunate; suffering with both can be dangerous. However, improvements can be made; even in a worst-case situation, safety and the enjoyability of trailering can be greatly improved.

WEIGHT AND BALANCE

Trailers are available in two types: conventional travel trailers and fifth-wheel trailers *(Figure 4.1)*. (Included in the travel-trailer category are folding camping trailers.) We will concentrate on the handling characteristics of conventional travel trailers here, since by design they are much more vulnerable to destabilizing forces than are fifth-wheels. That statement might suggest that fifth-wheel trailers are preferable. (Owners of fifth-wheels undoubtedly would agree.) However, travel trailers have many positive attributes, one of which is that various types of tow vehicles can be used. Also, when the popular pickup truck is utilized, its bed is not occupied by a hitch and by the trailer's front overhang, which greatly improves travel flexibility. With proper balance and hitch equipment, conventional travel trailers will handle properly and are safe.

The problem that can occur with travel trailers is a phenomenon called sway, technically known as yaw, which does not occur with fifth-wheel trailers. Sway is a fishtailing (sideways see-saw) action of the trailer caused by external forces that set the trailer's mass into lat-

Figure 4.1: Travel trailers are subject to sway, which can be controlled, while fifth-wheel trailers are not.

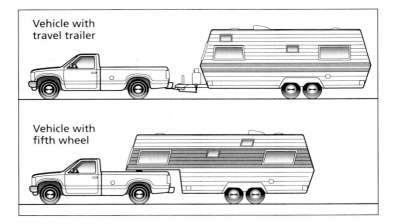

eral motion with the trailer's wheels serving as the axis or pivot point (*Figure 4.2*). All conventionally hitched travel trailers will sway slightly in response to crosswinds or the bow wave of an 18-wheeler overtaking from the rear. The good ones will need little correction by the driver and will quickly restabilize. Only poorly designed trailers will continue to sway after the force that caused the instability has ceased. In fact, the sway motion of a poorly balanced trailer may increase until control is lost.

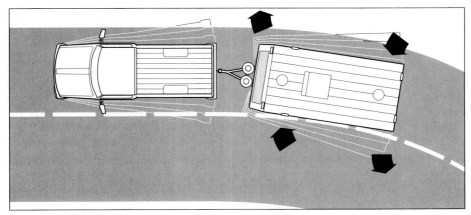

Figure 4.2: Lateral movement of a travel trailer exerts steering influence on the tow vehicle.

There are several ways to evaluate the potential of a travel trailer to sway and to correct the problem if it occurs.

STABILITY CHECKUP

A trailer's inherent stability is part of its design, based on the amount of weight in front of the axles versus the amount of weight behind. A weight-forward bias results in hitch weight *(Figure 4.3)* and is necessary for control. Trailers with insufficient hitch weight have two deficiencies:

1. The weight mass behind the axle(s) is too high; when set in

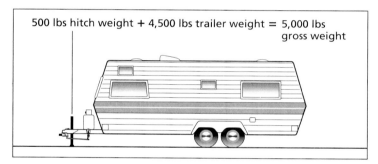

500 lbs hitch weight + 4,500 lbs trailer weight = 5,000 lbs gross weight

Figure 4.3: Proper travel trailer handling depends on balance, indicated by the proportion between hitch weight and gross weight

motion it acts as pendulum.

2. The distance between the hitch ball and the trailer axles is insufficient to give the tow vehicle steering leverage over the trailer.

Elementary physics helps explain why distance between the hitch ball and axles is important. We all know that we can use a board (lever) positioned on a rock (fulcrum) to move another rock that is too heavy for us to lift without assistance. The lever gives us a mechanical advantage (leverage) on the rock. Likewise, trailers that have considerably more length in front of their axle(s) than in the rear give tow vehicles a mechanical advantage: the tow vehicle has a long lever with which to steer the trailer. This balance question is dealt with in terms of pounds of hitch weight.

Simply stated, trailers with a high proportion of hitch weight to gross weight usually have more of their length ahead of the axles, and they handle better. The generally accepted industry standard is that hitch weight should be approximately 10 percent of gross weight. In fact, that is a bare minimum, and some trailers with 10 percent hitch weight don't handle well. Hitch weights of 12 percent or higher (up to the weight limits of the hitch being used) assure proper handling.

In marginal hitch-weight situations, the owner's ability to handle an unstable trailer will depend on the inherent stability of the tow vehicle, which is another variable. A truck or van with long wheelbase, relatively short rear overhang, and stiff springs will at least partially make up for a trailer's lack of inherent stability. But if the trailer is towed by a softly sprung truck or van or a passenger car, the trailer's shortcomings will be more obvious.

A brief driving test on a section of straight road with no other traffic in sight will give you an assessment of your trailer's inherent stability. The trial should be conducted with the tow vehicle and trailer loaded normally for travel. Make sure the refrigerator door is secured and that contents of cabinets will not be dislodged. If you have a friction-type sway-control device, set the adjusting lever so the device is not operational. A sway-control device is a valuable asset and should be employed, but for the purposes of this test, it should be disconnected so it does not camouflage inherent trailer instability.

For this trial, trailer brakes should be working effectively, and the manual control lever on the brake controller should be within easy reach of the driver *(Figure 4.4)*. If your brake controller does not have

Figure 4.4: The best emergency measure for control of sway is by activation of the trailer brakes via the lever on the controller.

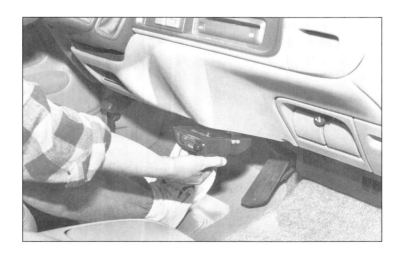

a lever that allows you to actuate trailer brakes independently of tow-vehicle brakes, it's important that you change to a controller that does. **Independent use of trailer brakes is the single most effective countermeasure to reduce or eliminate trailer sway.**

Begin the test at about twenty miles per hour and crank the steering wheel sharply to the left, simulating an attempt to avoid an obstacle in the road. Note the reaction of the trailer. Repeat the experiment while increasing speed, but take care not to overdo it. Practice actuating the trailer brakes independently of the tow-vehicle brakes so you can do it almost instinctively. As speeds increase, the trailer will sway more dramatically. With each trial, note the severity of trailer sway and how many oscillations occur before the trailer restabilizes. Again, take care not to exceed the limits of your tow vehicle and trailer.

The most pronounced sway oscillations should be the ones produced by your sharp steering input; subsequent oscillations should diminish rapidly. If the second and third sway oscillations are equally as severe or worse than the first, the trailer is unstable (or marginally stable at best) and needs correction. Don't be lulled into complacency by the fact that the trailer handles much better when your sway-control device is in use. Sure it does! But an emergency maneuver may overcome the effect of the sway-control unit and result in an accident.

HOW A TRAILER SHOULD HANDLE

Many trailerists become accustomed to being uncomfortable or even frightened by trailer sway when they encounter strong crosswinds, trucks overtaking them from the rear, or mountainous roads. They think it's normal—the way all trailers handle. Not so! Properly designed, well-matched tow vehicles and trailers have positive control and good road manners. Certainly, strong crosswinds may tend to push the tow vehicle/trailer combination laterally, and it may end up partially in the next lane if the driver isn't paying close attention. But the rig should be sufficiently controllable so that the driver can use corrective steering without being intimidated by sway. Likewise, it should be possible to drive a mountain road at brisk speeds while being able to keep the tow vehicle in the proper position on curves.

Speeding 18-wheelers present hazards to travel trailers that don't handle well, particularly while descending mountain grades. A tow vehicle/trailer rig is most susceptible to destabilizing forces while

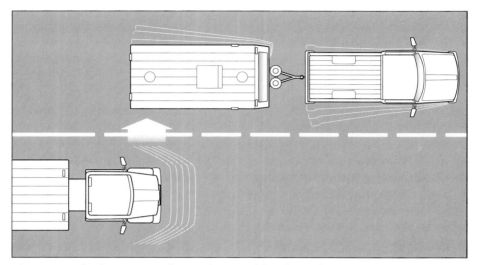

Figure 4.5: The bow wave of a truck overtaking from the rear may require defensive steering.

descending a grade at highway speeds, and such conditions are the true test of inherent stability.

It's natural for the bow wave (air pressure) of a speeding 18-wheeler to have an effect on a tow vehicle and trailer *(Figure 4.5)*, requiring steering correction. But the effect should not be sufficient destabilization that driving is uncomfortable or scary. A properly balanced rig will not handle that way, although it will always be necessary to monitor one's rear-view mirror and anticipate the effects of an 18-wheeler overtaking from the rear. Drivers of all kinds of high-profile vehicles must do this; drivers of marginally stable vehicles who are caught napping usually are the ones who get into trouble.

EVALUATING THE TRAILER AND HITCH

Even if your road trial produced good results, it's wise to check your trailer's weight and balance. The first step in evaluating a trailer for correction of stability is a trip to the scales *(see Chapter 1 for the proper weighing procedure)*. If your hitch-weight percentage is down around 10 percent (or less), it can explain a trailer's unstable behavior. If hitch weight is 11 to 13 percent, towing stability still could be a problem if the tow vehicle is marginally stable. If hitch weight is 12 to 15 percent, the trailer should handle well and not be the cause of an instability problem. Exceptions are trailers that have high weight masses, such as the water tank in the rear, serving as a pendulum and partially overcoming the relatively lengthy steering lever (distance between axles and hitch ball) that otherwise would assure good stability. Trailers with 15 to 20 percent hitch weight are even better, but it's important that the weight does not exceed the rating of the hitch, which ranges between 800 and 1,700 pounds, depending on brand and model. Hitch ratings are stamped on hitch receivers.

In Table 4.1, hitch weight is marginal but acceptable. This trailer

Table 4.1
Calculating Hitch-weight Percentage (Marginal–Acceptable)

Gross trailer weight	5,400 pounds
Hitch weight	620 pounds
Hitch-weight percentage	620 ÷ 5,400 = 11% (approximate)

Table 4.2
Calculating Hitch-weight Percentage (Not Acceptable)

Gross trailer weight	6,200 pounds
Hitch weight	550 pounds
Hitch-weight percentage	550 ÷ 6,200 = 9% (approximate)

should handle well behind a truck or van with a long wheelbase but may not be ideal behind a short-wheelbase sport utility vehicle.

Table 4.2 illustrates a trailer that clearly has insufficient hitch weight and is undoubtedly prone to sway.

The only solution is to move weight forward. This may be accomplished by relocating supplies or a rear-mounted spare tire. The worst place for a tire, or anything else that is relatively heavy, is on the back of the trailer. Carry it in the tow vehicle. Another possibility is the battery; if carried in the rear, it could be relocated to the trailer A-frame. The freshwater tank should not be located behind the trailer axles. This does occur, however, and when designers have properly compen-

Figure 4.6:
A friction-
sway-control
unit is essential
for the best
possible
trailer han-
dling.

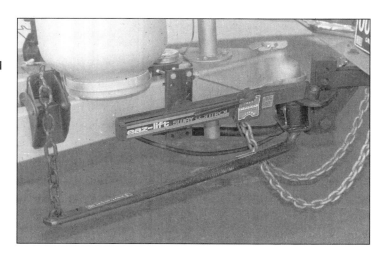

sated by assuring that hitch weight is adequate when the water tank is full, the trailer may handle reasonably well. If hitch weight is inadequate, a rear water tank may be replaced by one of a different shape that will fit under a sofa in the forward section of the trailer, the positive effect on stability will be dramatic. Ideally, the water tank should be located over the axles, so its varying content does not affect hitch weight. Of course, it's wise to empty holding tanks before traveling to minimize weight in the rear.

Assuming hitch weight is raised to at least 12 percent, the use of an effective sway control should give the trailer reasonably good road manners. Two types of sway controls are available: friction-type controls from Reese and Eaz-Lift *(Figure 4.6)* and the Reese Dual Cam Sway Control *(Figure 4.7)*. Both are effective, but since the Reese Dual Cam depends on adequate hitch weight for its effectiveness, it's most suitable to trailers with moderate to high hitch weights. Proper adjust-

Figure 4.7:
Reese Dual-
Cam sway
control uti-
lizes friction
between cams
and brackets
at the ends of
spring bars.

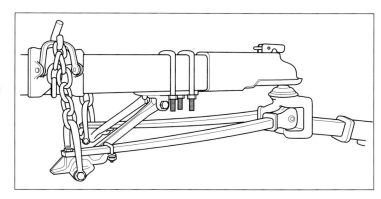

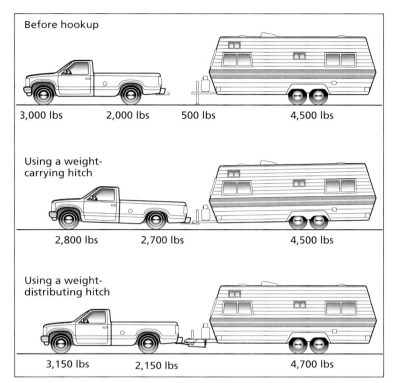

Figure 8.8: A weight-distributing hitch distributes weight to all axles of the tow vehicle and the trailer.

Before hookup

3,000 lbs   2,000 lbs   500 lbs   4,500 lbs

Using a weight-carrying hitch

2,800 lbs   2,700 lbs   4,500 lbs

Using a weight-distributing hitch

3,150 lbs   2,150 lbs   4,700 lbs

ment of the friction cams of the Dual Cam system also is very important for best stability. When it's not possible to achieve adequate hitch weight through relocation of supplies or appliances, two friction-type sway controls may be used as a stopgap measure.

PROPER HITCH ADJUSTMENT

Yet another important factor in tow vehicle/trailer stability is proper adjustment of a conventional load-distributing hitch. Proper adjustment means that the trailer is level and that the tow vehicle remains in the same attitude as before hitching. For example, if the tow vehicle was canted up at the rear before hitching (typical of pickup trucks), it should remain at that angle after hitching. The concept of a properly operating load-distributing hitch is that it should distribute hitch weight to all axles of the tow vehicle and trailer *(Figure 4.8)*.

To make certain this happens, follow these steps:

1. Measure the vehicle at reference points on front and rear
   bumpers with the vehicle loaded for travel but prior to hitching
   (Figure 4.9).
2. Hitch the trailer and adjust the spring-bar tension so weight
   appears to have been added to the front as well as the rear of the
   tow vehicle.
3. Remeasure the front and rear reference points. If, for example,
   the rear of the vehicle has dropped 1 inch and the front has only

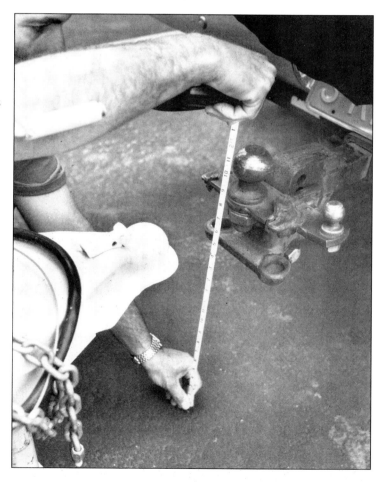

Figure 4.9:
Proper
adjustment of
spring-bar
tension is
based on
measurements
at front and
rear of tow
vehicle.

dropped ¼ inch, add more tension to the spring bars, which will raise the rear and lower the front. Continue adjusting until the measurements are approximately the same. If a discrepancy is unavoidable, the rear of the vehicle should drop slightly more than the front.

If the spring bars cannot be adjusted tight enough to achieve similar or identical vehicle-height reduction, stiffer spring bars may be needed. The spring bars should be rated for at least the amount of the hitch weight of the trailer, plus about 200 pounds if the tow vehicle is softly sprung. If, after proper adjustment of the tow-vehicle attitude, the trailer is not level, the ball mount should be raised or lowered. Adjustable ball mounts permit ball-height adjustment. If the ball mount is welded to the shank, replace it with an adjustable ball mount, available at most RV supply stores.

Sway-Control Adjustment

A sway control should be used, no matter how good trailer stability appears to be. The sway control dampens or slows the pivoting motion of the trailer coupler on the ball and is valuable during emergency maneuvers to counteract driver steering overreaction, not to mention its role in helping the tow vehicle and trailer to act in concert with each other.

With a friction-bar sway control, tighten the control until you notice that the tow vehicle doesn't quite straighten out after completing a sharp turn at slow speeds. Loosen the control a bit, to the point you feel comfortable. With the Reese Strait-Line sway control, the adjustment procedure involves driving straight forward very slowly while aiming the vehicle at a fixed object. Thus, with the tow vehicle and trailer in near-perfect longitudinal alignment, the sway-control brackets are centered over the friction cams. If the brackets aren't centered, loosen the hold-down bolts and move the cams forward or aft as necessary.

The Pullrite Hitch

Sway control is available in several forms, and one of the most effective devices is a very unconventional hitch called the PullRite *(Figure 4.10)*. The unique feature of this hitch is that it relocates the tow vehicle/trailer pivot point from its usual location behind the

Figure 4.10:
The unique
PullRite hitch
pivots under
the vehicle,
preventing
trailer sway.

bumper to a point immediately behind the rear axle. The trailer no longer pivots on the hitch ball, so it's necessary to visualize the trailer A-frame having been extended about five feet underneath the tow vehicle to the pivot point. With the trailer in effect, lengthened, a certain amount of maneuverability is sacrificed. The PullRite also functions as a load-distributing (equalizing) hitch.

The PullRite has a dramatic effect on towing stability. Even a basically unstable trailer is cured of its bad road manners. The principle is similar to that of fifth-wheel hitching, although the applications differ widely. The fifth-wheel hitch pin normally is positioned a couple of inches ahead of the rear-axle center line, topside in the bed of the truck, while the PullRite pivot point is underneath the vehicle, a few inches to the rear of the axle housing. Results are similar; on the road, directional control of the tow vehicle is not significantly affected by the steering forces of a marginally stable trailer.

The PullRite also differs from conventional load-distributing hitches in the amount of hardware installed under the tow vehicle. The PullRite utilizes a long draw bar and a radius bar, adding about sixty pounds beyond the weight of a conventional hitch receiver. The draw bar extends eleven inches behind the vehicle's bumper when the bar is straight to the rear. It can be swung out of the way when the hitch is not in use and locked in a stored position at the right rear corner of the unit.

While making turns, the PullRite causes the trailer to follow the tow vehicle farther toward the inside of the turn, similar to the way a fifth-wheel trailer behaves. This requires some relearning by the driver to keep from towing the trailer over curbs and into obstacles.

The Hensley Arrow

Another very effective stabilizing trailer hitch is the Hensley Arrow *(Figure 4.11)*. It's a fairly complex system, part of which replaces the conventional hitch-ball mount; the remainder of the system is attached to the trailer coupler and A-frame.

The system uses linkages to, in effect, make a virtually solid linkup between tow vehicle and trailer while traveling in a straight course. The hitch functions as if all of the normal pivoting action of the coupler on the ball is gone—making the tow vehicle and trailer function as though they are linked solidly. Thus, any tendency of the trailer to sway is not applied as steering force on the tow vehicle. But amazingly, when the driver wants to turn, the linkages permit a normal turn. The result is a system that eliminates trailer sway.

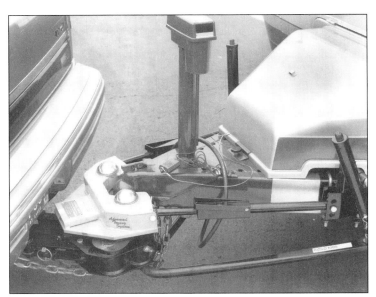

Figure 4.11: The Hensley Arrow locks the tow vehicle and trailer in a straight-ahead position; any tendency of the trailer to sway is not applied as steering force on the tow vehicle.

The Hensley system consists of many components but is suitable for installation by the owner. Once the system is installed, hitching is simplified. All the components stay with the trailer when the tow vehicle is unhitched. Rehitching involves backing the tow vehicle's hitch receiver onto the hitch bar shank, which requires practice before it becomes routine.

Evaluating the Tow Vehicle

Tow vehicles come in all shapes and sizes and with varying inherent stability for trailer towing. Factors that affect stability include wheelbase length, rear overhang, steering characteristics, and center of gravity. The most significant factor is the proportion between the wheelbase and rear overhang *(Figure 4.12)*. A longer wheelbase makes a vehicle respond more slowly to steering input. A short rear overhang gives the trailer less mechanical advantage over the tow vehicle. The combination of the two—long wheelbase and short rear overhang—provides the greatest stability. These two proportions are usually best in vans.

Typically, older short-wheelbase sport utility vehicles are not as stable as are vans, trucks, and Suburbans built by the same manufacturers. Late-model versions such as the Ford Expedition and GM Tahoe/Yukon with longer wheelbases and much more sophisticated suspensions, are excellent tow vehicles. In particular, the Ford

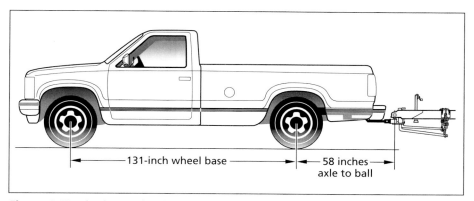

131-inch wheel base ——————→←— 58 inches ——→
axle to ball

Figure 4.12: The long wheelbase and short rear overhang provide excellent resistance to trailer instability.

Expedition has a very good proportion between wheelbase and rear overhang.

If sway tends to be a problem even though the trailer has a good proportion of hitch weight versus gross weight and hitching is proper, it may be necessary to raise the trailer's hitch-weight proportion still higher. The sway-control device being utilized should be very effective. If a Reese Strait-Line is used with a trailer that has less than 12 to 15 percent hitch weight, it may be necessary to add a friction-type sway control and use both sway-control devices.

For the tow vehicle itself, use the air pressure (molded on tire sidewalls) in rear tires to stiffen their sidewalls; use the vehicle manufacturer's recommended pressure in front. Use good-quality gas-pressure shock absorbers, which tend to keep the vehicle in better control on unlevel road surfaces. If the vehicle responds too quickly to steering input, have an alignment shop set the front end to the manufacturer's maximum positive caster setting. Additional caster tends to reduce steering response. A friction-type sway control adjusted to a stiff setting is especially important for comfortable towing with four-wheel-drive sport utility vehicles.

Fifth-Wheel Towing

Directional stability with fifth-wheel trailers is usually so good that it's hardly worth discussing. Only in cases where the fifth-wheel hitch pin is located behind the center line of the truck's rear axle does stability become a factor, and even then it's rarely a problem.

Safety factors that definitely are worth discussing include secure attachment of the hitch, proper attention while hitching, assuring the pin is securely locked in the coupler, proper tire pressures, and proper tire/wheel compatibility.

Fifth-wheel hitches should be bolted through the truck bed to the truck frame for rigidity. If there is any doubt about your installation, contact the manufacturer of your hitch and ask for installation instructions.

Maintenance of proper tire pressures is important with any vehicle, but especially for large trailers. Low tire pressures, even for just a few hours, can cause insidious damage that can lead to a blowout later, when the low-pressure incident is long forgotten and there appears to be no explanation for the tire failure. Also, especially with the larger fifth-wheel trailers, wheel suitability may be questionable. This is particularly the case with styled wheels, many of which are rated for 2,000 to 2,200 pounds each and forty psi maximum pressure, whereas the tire may be rated for considerably more weight as well as pressure. See Chapter 7 for more information on tire/wheel suitability.

Freeway Hop

A bouncing, jerking motion commonly known as freeway hop occurs in some trailer rigs enough to become uncomfortable. The problem is very difficult to solve, even though it has existed for many years. It's caused by poor highway design—unfortunate spacing of the seams in the concrete (typically, fifteen-foot sections) so they set up a rhythmic bounce that reverberates throughout the tow vehicle and trailer *(Figure 4.13)*. Whether or not it happens—and in what severity—depends on the spacing of tow vehicle and trailer axles and how they strike the pavement seams.

Theoretically, changing the distance between tow vehicle and trailer axles should have an effect. However, the amount of that effect is impossible to predict. The simple way to change this distance is to extend the ball three to four inches farther behind the bumper. This can be done by changing to a longer hitch bar. The downside of this is that extension of the hitch can adversely affect towing stability.

Short of the hitch length change, good shocks and 1,000-pound hitch spring bars are recommended. Another change that improves some rigs and not others is the addition of shock absorbers to the trailer (assuming it does not already have them). Check with the manufacturer of your trailer chassis to see if a shock-absorber-parts kit is available.

Changing to better shock absorbers for the tow vehicle, although of benefit for overall vehicle handling, does not appear to solve the bounce problem.

CORRECTIVE DRIVING TECHNIQUES

The best defense against sway is a good offense—correction of weight distribution, proper hitching, and use of a good sway control. If stability still occasionally becomes marginal under exceptionally bad

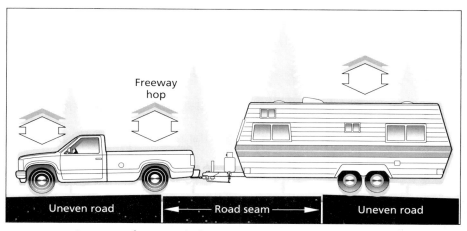

Figure 4.13: Improper freeway design can cause a rhythmic bouncing of the tow vehicle and trailer.

driving conditions, the driver must compensate by reducing speed, which will slow the reaction of the vehicle to external forces and allow you more time to react.

When sway occurs, by far the best technique for counteracting it is independent actuation of trailer brakes, even though it requires removing one hand from the steering wheel. In an emergency situation, this may require good self-control. But the driver who is vigilant about monitoring driving conditions and the scene in his rear-view mirror will anticipate a destabilizing situation and be prepared to use defensive techniques so the situation does not get out of control.

Although few hitch shops give it much thought, the location of the brake controller is a critical safety consideration. If it's positioned far under the dash and is hard to reach, relocate it to a better position, accessible to the hand you can most comfortably remove from the steering wheel—usually the left hand. With a properly balanced rig, you probably won't need to use the manual brake-control lever. But being capable of using it is your insurance policy against loss of control in an emergency situation involving trailer sway.

If severe sway occurs, don't step on the tow-vehicle brake pedal unless you're in danger of hitting something. Just lift your foot from the accelerator pedal and apply trailer brakes sharply via the hand control. During adverse driving conditions such as severe crosswinds, reduce speed and anticipate terrain that can produce sharp wind blasts. Be prepared to use trailer brakes if necessary.

This discussion of defensive tactics may sound severe and discouraging to travel-trailer ownership. In fact, proper towing setup involving a travel trailer can be just as enjoyable as towing a fifth-wheel with few, if any, anxious moments. But it does require proper attention paid to tow vehicle suitability, trailer balance, and correct hitching combined with a knowledge of defensive measures.

EQUIPMENT MAINTENANCE

Maintenance procedures for tow-vehicle chassis usually are very clearly defined in owners' manuals. In contrast, few trailer manufacturers offer advice on chassis maintenance.

In fact, very little is necessary, except for trailer brakes and bearings, which should be checked once a year, prior to the travel season, or more often if the trailer is towed long distances in mountainous terrain. Electric-brake components may wear rapidly under such conditions, and hubs should be removed to check the condition of the magnets, armature, and brake shoes. Wheel bearings should be repacked and grease seals should be changed when such inspections are performed.

However, regular inspection is necessary because trailer springs and particularly shackles—the brackets that attach the springs to the trailer axles and frame—are subject to wear. Make it a point to regularly inspect the shackles as well as the bolts used to secure them. Since shackles often become elongated, check them at the bolt holes and replace any that have elongated holes. Also check for spring wear and breakage. If a trip over exceptionally rough roads is planned, buy a couple of spring leaves for use in emergencies. When replacing spring shackles, use a replacement kit made by Dexter Axle Company that includes grease fittings, which extend repair intervals.

By evaluating trailer stability and taking the proper steps to assure better handling, towing travel trailers can be much more enjoyable.

TIPS THAT WORK

Help from History

Have you ever forgotten to retract your RV step before starting down the road? I did once, but fortunately didn't hit anything, or cause the expensive damage that I know is possible.

Using nothing more than a metal coat hanger, a bolt, a nut, and a washer, I came up with a simple and inexpensive way to prevent this potentially serious oversight. Do you remember the curb feelers that were introduced for use on automobiles in the 1950s? My little modification is a design variation of that idea.

Start by cutting and bending the hanger as needed to make sure that it reaches the ground whenever the step is down. Drill a ¼-inch hole in the outer corner of the step, bend a small loop on the end of the wire that will attach to the step, and maybe another in the middle to act as a spring. Secure the device in place using a ¼-inch bolt, nut and lockwasher. It's best to use a brass or stainless steel bolt that won't rust. Finish by making certain that the wire does not extend into foot-path traffic or touch the ground when the step is retracted.

Now, if you ever try to pull away without stowing the RV entry step, your new step feeler will save the day by dragging loudly and distinctly against the pavement to alert you.

If you want to get fancy, a chrome-plated hanger or a standard curb feeler can be used for a custom look.

Richard A. Richey
Clinton, OH

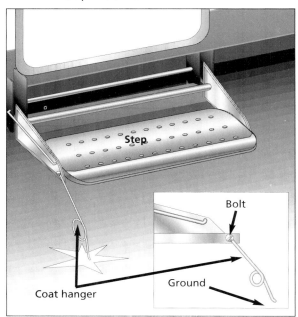

Improving Fuel Economy and Performance

In this chapter the following items will be covered:

- Aftermarket Mileage and Performance Products
- Evaluating Engine Condition
- Tests That Require Teardown
- Aftermarket Modifications
- On the Road
- Hill Climbing and Passing

*M*ost RV owners range from very interested to mildly obsessed with fuel economy. Even though we may be able to afford to travel in a vehicle that gets 6 to 10 MPG, we're not satisfied with it; somehow, we thought mileage would be better.

Unfortunately, it takes considerable amounts of fuel to move large, heavy, aerodynamically challenged vehicles. Vehicle manufacturers have pursued technological advances such as computerized engine-management systems and electronically controlled overdrives, and the effort has paid off. New engine designs have proven to be consistently more fuel miserly than the engines they replaced. For example, when GM introduced the Vortec engines in 1996, they used noticeably less fuel than their predecessors. Likewise, Ford's 6.8-liter V-10 has been a significant improvement over the 7.5-liter V-8.

For those of us who are not prone to trade up and acquire the newer technology there are steps we can take to make the best of what we have: increase the efficiency of the drivetrain and reduce wind resistance, rolling resistance, and weight. Any improvements made in these categories should yield increases in performance.

AFTERMARKET PRODUCTS TO ENHANCE MILEAGE AND PERFORMANCE

The automotive aftermarket offers a vast array of products that enhance mileage and performance, including aerodynamic aids, exhaust systems with low-restriction mufflers, reprogrammed engine computers or chips, fresh-air intake systems, custom intake manifolds, high-performance ignition systems, RV cams, roller rocker arms and lifters, special spark plugs, energy-conserving oils and oil additives, low-rolling-resistance tires, and many more.

In order to visualize changes to a powerplant, consider that internal combustion engines are basically air pumps. Modifications should attempt to improve the efficiency of the engine. At the risk of oversimplification, anything that makes it easier for air to get through the engine should yield higher output (assuming the correct amount of fuel gets mixed with it). Improvements in efficiency can be used to make the vehicle accelerate quicker and climb hills faster or to reduce fuel consumption while driving at the same speeds as before.

It may be difficult to separate the valid systems from those that produce little, if any, improvement, but some products offer significant advances. However, the mileage and performance claims made by manufacturers of some products are exaggerated and sometimes even ridiculous.

Is it "Smog" Legal?

While some of the products can correct factory deficiencies, they may conflict with emission laws. Enforcement of such laws has grown more thorough, and it is best to make sure that any engine modification is emission legal. Products that have a California Air Resources Board (CARB) exemption or Executive Order (EO) number are legal for use on the emission-controlled vehicles they are intended for in all states. However, this only indicates that emissions were not significantly affected; it does not certify that the product will improve performance or economy.

Because few products designed to improve fuel economy actually meet their advertising claims, the RV owner is wise to examine such products very carefully—especially in areas with strict emission regulations. Check closely on refund and warranty policies as well as the company's reputation. While the manufacturer of a miracle gas-saver gadget may offer what appears to be a very solid customer-satisfaction money-back guarantee, actually getting a refund may be difficult or impossible.

While some engines have deficiencies that can be corrected with aftermarket products, the more common problem is that the engine may be suffering from premature power loss although it's not ready for a complete overhaul. Most of us are aware of basic preventive-maintenance procedures; we change our oil every 3,000 miles and take it for granted that the engine should last for 100,000 miles. However, as we approach the halfway mark on the odometer, we may already begin to notice subtle signs of fatigue-reduced throttle response, more tendency to spark knock, and an increase in oil consumption.

This chapter will use two approaches to analyze fuel economy and performance:

1. How to make the best of what you have by making sure the engine meets its full potential.
2. How to correct an engine's factory deficiencies with cost-effective modifications, if available.

First, let's have a look at causes of engine-efficiency losses and discuss how to measure such losses.

EVALUATING ENGINE CONDITION

Timing Chains

Many engines begin to show signs of fatigue by the time odometer mileage reaches 50,000 miles. Engine-fatigue signals usually include reduction in fuel mileage, a change in cranking compression (variance between cylinders of more than 10 percent), a reduction in acceleration and hill-climbing ability, an increase in the engine's tendency to spark knock, and/or a tendency to run hotter. Oil consumption may also increase.

A primary cause of mileage and performance deterioration early in an engine's life cycle is wear of the timing chain (*Figure 5.1*). This chain's role is to turn the camshaft and in many cases, the distributor

Figure 5.1: The timing chain is the engine component most vulnerable to premature wear, which will retard cam timing and reduce fuel economy and performance.

and oil pump. As wear occurs in the chain's links, it lengthens, and camshaft timing is retarded, thereby reducing performance and mileage. Continued timing-chain wear will eventually result in the failure of the timing-chain assembly.

In most cases, timing-chain wear is within acceptable limits until the mid-century mark. By the time the vehicle accumulates upwards of 100,000 miles, most timing-chain assemblies should be replaced. Timing chains on the Dodge 5.9-liter and Ford 7.5-liter engines and GM engines with plastic cam-gear teeth may need replacement even earlier.

Premium-quality double-row timing-chain assemblies should be used in all applications. Timing-chain wear can be checked by using this simple procedure:

1. Remove the spark plugs and distributor cap, and rotate the engine by using a wrench on the crankshaft nut.
2. Turn the engine in the opposite direction of the spark-timing scale until you reach top dead center.
3. Ask an assistant to observe the distributor rotor. Rotate the engine, and watch the timing mark as it moves up the scale. When the assistant notices that the distributor rotor is beginning to move, stop turning the crankshaft and note the number of degrees of crankshaft rotation.

This number of degrees relative to movement of the rotor is a measure of timing-chain lash. Lash in excess of four degrees will begin to affect performance. At eight degrees, the loss in performance will become evident, and at twelve degrees the timing-chain assembly is nearing failure and should definitely be replaced. Failure of a timing chain often causes major engine damage when pistons strike the valves.

Fuel Injectors

Fuel injectors must spray a very fine mist of fuel into the engine *(Figure 5.2)*. Over time, this mist spray pattern deteriorates because solid deposits from the fuel build up inside the nozzles until the engine begins to run roughly. Power, fuel economy, and emissions suffer.

Modern fuels contain additives that retard the formation of deposits; fuel injectors on late-model vehicles are designed to resist clogging. However, this problem can still occur, and it happens so slowly that a person who drives the vehicle regularly won't notice the decline in perfomance.

On gasoline engines, injector clogging usually manifests itself as a "lumpy" idle, surging, hesitation, and, in bad cases, as a slight misfire. Diesel engines may make an unusual knocking or pinging sound under light accelerator settings and may produce more black smoke than normal or even make some white smoke.

Most gasoline and diesel-fuel injectors can be cleaned and tested and returned to service. Sometimes they leak or are damaged, in which case they can be replaced by new or rebuilt units.

Unfortunately, it's not easy to be sure a drivability problem is caused by injector deposits without removing them and bench-testing each one. Slightly clogged injectors are not detected by conventional diagnostic equipment. Many shops decide to check the injectors when the other systems check out okay, but the engine still doesn't run properly.

However, there are some guidelines to help you to know when to suspect injector problems. Generally, injector clogging doesn't occur at very low mileages. Before replacing injectors, make sure the engine is properly tuned and the compression is up to specifications and is

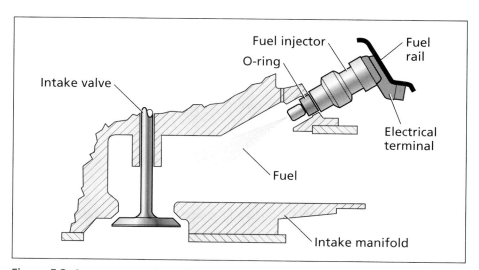

Figure 5.2: Spray pattern from fuel injectors may deteriorate with time, due to deposits in the injectors and must be cleaned or replaced.

uniform. Insure that ignition cables are in good condition and all fuel and air filters are clean. Also see if the "check engine" light is on or any computer trouble codes are stored in memory.

Injectors may be chemically cleaned on the vehicle. This can be done with chemicals added to the fuel tank or by connecting a special apparatus to feed the chemical directly to the injectors in place of fuel. The engine is then operated until the cleaner is consumed in the combustion process.

Additives placed in the fuel tank are greatly diluted and therefore less effective than the concentrated direct chemical feed to the fuel line. This latter method can be effective and is less expensive than removing injectors. The drawback is that it provides no method of testing the degree of clogging or the success of the cleaning process.

Some fuel-injection specialists have off-the-vehicle injector cleaning and test machines. These units are the costliest but most accurate method of servicing injectors. Injectors can be flow-tested before and after cleaning, and the volume and spray pattern can be checked. Injectors can be matched for flow rate, and any injectors that fail the tests may be replaced.

Figure 5.3: Poor performance and fuel economy may indicate low cylinder compression, which should not vary more than 10 percent from one cylinder to another.

Cylinder Pressure

When performance or mileage begins to sag, a compression test is in order. Always perform compression tests with the throttle held open, and allow two or three compression strokes of each piston being tested. Compression readings should not vary more than about 10 percent between cylinders *(Figure 5.3)*. If a higher variance is noted, inject a few squirts of motor oil into the low cylinder and into the one adjacent to it, then retest both. If the retest figures show that the cylinders are closer in compression, this indicates ring sealing is a problem. If cylinder balance remains about the same as the first test, a valve-leaking problem is indicated. When a piston-ring problem is indicated, recheck the compression after changing the oil and driving for about 100 miles. In some cases, rings may be sticking or a cylinder wall may have been washed down due to excessive fuel from a cold start *(see Chapter 6)*.

Oil Consumption

The amount of oil used by an engine is directly related to how the engine is used—i.e., heavy or severe service will result in higher oil consumption than occurs with less stringent use. The rate is roughly proportional to fuel consumption, which usually is a direct indicator of how hard the engine is working.

Ford's "Motorhome Chassis Service Manual" notes that vehicles over 8,500 pounds GVWR should go at least 900 miles per quart of oil, but that vehicles subject to severe duty may use more oil.

GM's recommendation for the Mark 4 version of their 7.4-liter engine (454 cid) used in motorhome chassis was very liberal for many years; a quart at 250 to 500 miles was considered normal for a motorhome engine. But oil consumption expectation for the Generation V version of the 7.4-liter engine, introduced in 1991 with improved oil seals, is more conservative. A GM engineer described as acceptable the use of a quart for every 150 gallons of fuel consumed. At that rate, a vehicle getting 7 MPG would go about 1,000 miles per quart of oil consumed.

Keep a record of mileage points at which oil is added and a list of oil changes by date and odometer mileage so you can have an accurate reading of the engine's oil consumption. In addition to the natural consumption of oil past the piston rings, leakage through valve guides and seals is common in older engines.

There are two other methods of determining if oil is passing through the valve guides or past the intake manifold. After shutting down a hot engine and allowing it to sit for thirty minutes, restart the engine without using the throttle. Observe the tailpipe; if blue smoke is emitted upon startup, the oil is more likely passing through the valve guides and seals than leaking past an intake-manifold gasket.

Another method is to check for oil smoke after coasting down a long grade and applying throttle at the bottom. Oil smoke will increase immediately upon applying throttle and will disappear or greatly reduce in a few seconds if continued throttle is applied.

If uncorrected, excessive oil consumption can create carbon buildup in the combustion chambers and may foul spark plugs, causing misfire. This will result in further loss of power and economy and an increase in exhaust emissions.

Crankcase Pressure

When engine wear is suspected, it's advisable to check for excessive crankcase "blowby," which indicates combustion leakage past the pistons and rings. One method of checking this is:

1. Bring the engine to normal operating temperature.
2. Place the automatic transmission in park or the manual gearbox in neutral.
3. Apply the parking brake.
4. Block the wheels.
5. Remove the oil-fill cap.
6. Run the engine at approximately 2,500 rpm. If a substantial flow of oil vapors appear from the oil-fill opening, the pistons and/or rings are not sealing properly.
7. If the oil vapors are light, chances are that valve seals or guides are causing the excessive oil consumption.

If you are unsure of how much vapor should be present, perform this test on a known, well-functioning engine for familiarization.

Cylinder Leakdown Tests

Prior to engine teardown, always have a cylinder leakdown test performed. This test injects air pressure into each cylinder with the valves closed and measures the rate at which it escapes, expressed as a percentage. It will also pinpoint leaky valves or pistons/cylinders; the sound of air escaping through the intake manifold indicates intake valves are leaking; if it escapes out the tailpipe, exhaust valves are the cause, and if hissing can be heard in the oil-filler tube it means piston rings are worn.

Oil Pressure Test

If low oil pressure is a concern, double-check the stock gauge or light by temporarily using an aftermarket mechanical oil-pressure gauge. Checking with such a gauge will eliminate the chance of having a faulty sending unit or a voltage problem giving a false reading.

Distributor Function

Fully electronic ignition systems have eliminated the distributor on many engines, but malfunction of the distributor is among the many causes of premature power loss on vehicles with conventional distrib-

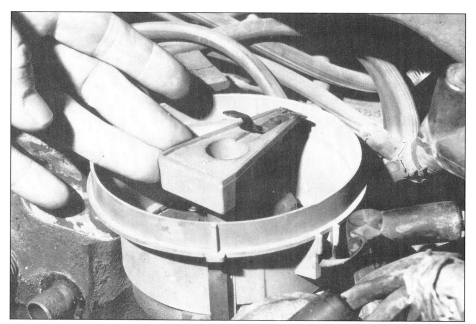

Figure 5.4: After twisting distributor rotor against spring tension, it should freely return to its original position.

utors. This was particularly the case with General Motors trucks and motorhome chassis up to the late 1980s, which used a system of mechanical spark-advance weights in a distributor that had an inner shaft that tended to bind. This caused the automatic spark-advance system to stick, resulting in power and mileage loss and/or starter kickback and pinging.

On vehicles with conventional distributors, the automatic spark-advance system is easy to check. To do so, just remove the distributor cap and twist the rotor against spring tension *(Figure 5.4)*. Spring tension on the centrifugal advance weights should return the rotor fully to the rest position. If it does not, the distributor must be disassembled, cleaned with solvent and fine emery paper, relubricated, and reinstalled.

To verify if your distributor doesn't have mechanical weights, read the emission-control label. If it indicates that ignition timing is nonadjustable, it won't have mechanical advance weights.

Most late-model vehicles no longer have vacuum spark-advance systems, but if yours does (a diaphragm attached to the distributor with a vacuum line connected to it), idle the engine and temporarily make and break the vacuum-line connection (using a source of manifold vacuum). You should be able to easily notice a difference in engine rpm as the vacuum advance affects spark timing.

Inspect the distributor cap and rotor for evidence of carbon tracking (leakage of electrical current). Don't be concerned that the tip of the rotor or the electrical contacts inside the cap appear to be burned; it's not advisable to clean the carbon from those surfaces. Use a light coat of electrical silicone compound instead. Although silicone is an insulator, it does not impair the distributor's function, and it prevents burning of the contact surfaces.

Take the vehicle to a local auto-repair shop equipped with an oscilloscope and have a mechanic check the secondary ignition system (spark plugs and spark-plug cables). These components are a common source of engine problems. Make sure the mechanic loads the engine (running engine in gear, foot on brake, and hand brake set) while checking for secondary electrical-ignition breakdown. This checkup will show bad spark-plug cables, spark plugs, or other ignition components. Primary voltage should be checked, especially on Chrysler vehicles.

TIPS THAT WORK

Shipshape Shaft

The ignition distributor in the GM 454 V-8 has a two-piece shaft that is part of the mechanical spark-advance system. If these two parts are not free to rotate several degrees, one within the other, the ignition timing will not be correct.

The problem should be corrected quickly, because it can affect starting, as well as contribute to pinging, reduced fuel economy, and poor overall engine performance.

The distributor cap must be removed to check for relative freedom of movement between the two shafts. Grip the rotor and try to rotate the top shaft against the pull of the centrifugal advance springs.

If movement is evident, remove the rotor and sparingly lubricate the mechanical linkage with 30-weight motor oil. Don't forget the felt wiper, if your distributor has one. Reinstall the rotor and cap, making sure that both are squarely and firmly seated.

If you can't induce movement, or if the rotor will not return to its normal position, remove the rotor and spray the center shaft with WD-40 while working it back and forth. If this loosens the advance mechanism, wipe off the excess spray lube, then oil it, as described earlier. Replace the rotor and cap, and check the initial ignition timing with a timing light.

Sometimes, however, the two shafts cannot be freed in this manner. If this is the case, have the distributor removed and repaired by a qualified mechanic.

George Taylor
Muscle Shoals, AL

Carburetor Function

Late-model RV engines all have been converted to electronic fuel injection, for which troubleshooting is covered in Chapter 8, but carburetors were used on some vehicles, including motorhomes, into the late 1980s. Most use nitrophyl (plastic) fuel-bowl floats, which gradually become saturated with fuel, raising the fuel level. The floats should be replaced every two years. An increase in weight compared to a new float is an indication of float saturation. The saturation causes excessive fuel use, stalling on corners and on abrupt stops, and hard starts while the engine is running hot.

Holley carburetors, common on Ford engines of the early and mid-1980s, use power valves for fuel enrichment. Internal-gasket failure,

Figure 5.5: A drinking straw inserted in the fuel bowl vent can be used to indicate metering-rod movement in the Quadrajet carburetor.

vacuum leaks, and backfiring of the engine through the carburetor can cause the valves to leak. To check for leakage, bring the engine to operating temperature, shut it down, and allow it to sit for thirty minutes. Without touching the accelerator pedal, have an assistant start the engine while you watch for excessive black smoke, indicating a faulty power valve. Excessive fuel consumption is another indication. Use of a Holley 6.5 power valve and new gaskets for the metering body and fuel bowl are advisable.

Improper operation of the choke can adversely affect engine performance, as well as reduce engine life. An over-rich choke allows excessive fuel to wash cylinder walls, causing accelerated wear. It also loads the spark plugs with carbon.

Most carburetors have choke systems with pull-off diaphragms that open the choke when the engine starts. These vacuum-operated diaphragms are fairly easy to check and adjust. The choke diaphragm is located on the outside of the carburetor and is connected via linkage to the choke butterfly. Before a cold startup, remove the air cleaner and observe the linkage that opens the butterfly. Start the engine to check that the linkage partially opens the butterfly immediately. If the diaphragm is faulty, remove it and take it to a parts supplier for visual confirmation that the new part you are buying is the same as the old one. The choke should progressively open and be fully open when the engine is up to operating temperature.

Metering-rod movement should be checked. Rods are externally accessible on some Carter carburetor models and can be checked to make sure they are not sticking. In Quadrajet four-barrel carburetors used on General Motors vehicles, a piece of drinking straw inserted into the fuel-bowl vent will come to rest on the top of the metering-rod piston *(Figure 5.5)*. When the engine starts, the piston will be drawn down and less of the straw will be visible. When the engine is shut down, the straw will rise. Under load, the metering rods should begin to rise at about 6.5 inches of manifold vacuum, which will be indicated by the position of the straw. A vacuum gauge can be used to test this function while running the engine in gear against the foot and hand brakes.

Secondary metering tubes in Quadrajet carburetors tend to loosen and drop into the secondary fuel bowl, causing a lean condition and power loss during heavy throttle. Checking for this problem requires the removal of the air horn (top) of the carburetor; the tubes are pressed into the air horn. If they have dropped out, reinsert them with a light coat of epoxy glue to hold them in place.

Also, check pressed-in plugs in the bottom of the fuel bowl for evidence of leakage. Layer epoxy glue on top of the plugs if leakage is suspected.

Fuel Volume and Pressure

Adequate fuel volume and pressure must be available whether the vehicle is fuel injected or carbureted. Check fuel filters; you should be able to blow freely through them. Fuel starvation can exist, creating a lean condition under a sustained load, without clear indication to the driver. This is especially true of fuel-injected engines. Fuel pressure and volume specifications are listed in shop manuals, along with testing procedures.

Generally, with carbureted engines, if volume is okay, pressure is acceptable. The fuel pump of a carbureted engine should produce a pint of fuel under free-flow conditions in fifteen to twenty seconds. Check the factory specifications for fuel-injected engines *(see Chapter 8)*. Sometimes fuel-injected engines have two pumps and only one will fail. This leads to drivability problems, such as stalling or surging, and may mimic vapor lock.

Air Filter

Inadequate fuel pressure, restricted filters, and other problems usually will be identified by the computerized codes. Beyond these items, it's especially important to make sure the air filter is in good condition.

In fuel-injected engines, proper maintenance of the air filter is crucial, especially on engines where fresh-air ducting is used. Although carbureted engines are also affected by restricted air filters, filter maintenance is much more critical in fuel-injected engines because fuel flow is controlled mainly by throttle position rather than airflow through venturi of a carburetor. Therefore, any restrictions in the air filter will dramatically affect fuel mileage. The air-filter element should be inspected every 10,000 miles. Also, look for restrictions in the fresh-air inlet tube. Hoses sometimes collapse, and foreign matter can partially block the inlet.

Valves

General Motors V-8s have adjustable valve lash, and they should be checked about every 20,000 miles. Valves of other popular V-8 RV engines are not adjustable. After valves are initially adjusted, audible valve noise is an indication of valve-train problems. Set GM valve adjustment to one-quarter turn down from zero lash, rather than the one full turn recommended by the factory. The valves should be adjusted with the engine idling. Rocker-arm adjusting nuts on GM vehicles are the friction type; be sure there is resistance to turning during the adjustment procedure. If no resistance is felt, replace the nut.

With the valve covers off, visually compare the movement or lift of one valve stem with another. They should be uniform. If one is low, it indicates a worn cam lobe or a bad lifter. Worn lobes are especially common with small-block Chevy engines. Compression checks performed with each tune-up will provide information about overall valve condition.

TESTS THAT REQUIRE TEARDOWN

Cylinder-Wall Taper

When substantial oil consumption is a problem and a leak-down test indicates faulty pistons/rings or walls, cylinder-wall taper should be checked. This requires the removal of the cylinder heads. If less than 0.004 inch of taper (wear) is found, proper honing of the cylinders and installation of moly piston rings may extend engine life.

Rod bearings should be inspected and may need to be replaced; piston-pin fit and connecting-rod alignment should also be checked. The main bearings should be inspected, but they seldom need replacement. Valve lifters should be removed (keep them in proper order for replacement in their original positions) to permit visual inspection of the camshaft. The engine should be rotated so all cam lobes can be inspected for pitting and wear. The bottom of each lifter should also be inspected for wear and pitting.

Manifold Inspection

During the process of checking cylinder-wall taper, also inspect the intake manifold. Observe the gasket surface at the lower side of each intake port for signs of oil leakage past the gasket. Faulty gaskets and/or improper torquing are common causes of this problem.

Check for manifold warpage. Thoroughly clean the manifold and place a light coat of oil on the surface contact areas. Cover the contact areas with a piece of glass. The coat of oil will contact the glass, and any warped areas will be evident because the oil will not adhere evenly to the glass. A warped manifold must be replaced.

The manifold must also be inspected for cracks. Having the manifold professionally cleaned and inspected is an excellent practice. If oil leakage past the intake gaskets is discovered, use particular care with the gaskets and sealant during reinstallation. First, use an effective gasket sealer/adhesive over the cylinder-head surfaces after these surfaces have been thoroughly cleaned. Put the gasket in place. Prior to installation of the manifold, apply a light coat of silicone sealer around each port and in each corner of the gasket. Immediately install the manifold, and torque to factory specifications.

If the valve seals must be replaced on a high-mileage engine, the heads should be disassembled and the guides should be remachined to accept Teflon-type free-floating seals. Pioneer and Perfect Circle are

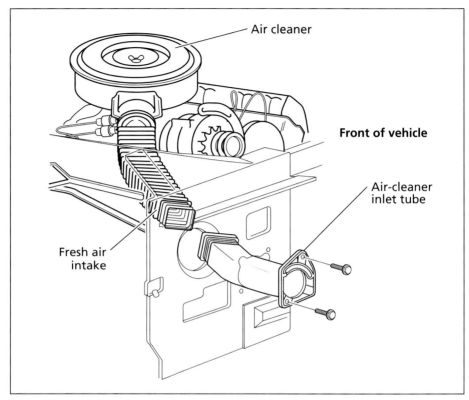

Figure 5.6: Unobstructed engine air intake should be positioned ahead of the radiator to avoid preheating.

two effective brands, available at auto-parts stores. These seals are to be used along with the standard seal. With the heads off the engine and all of the carbon removed, it's also logical to perform a valve job.

AFTERMARKET MODIFICATIONS

Properly selected aftermarket engine modifications can increase the efficiency and durability of the engine and drivetrain. The net result can be more power and/or better fuel economy. It's important to select components that work together. For example, if a higher-output camshaft is selected, it's important to have low-restriction intake and exhaust systems to go with it.

Air Intake

Air ducting designed to feed an engine intake from ahead of the radiator rather than the air preheated by the radiator is standard on most late-model engines and is essential for engine performance in hot weather. Such a system can be added to an older engine if it was not standard. An engine will perform better on cool air, which is denser than hot air *(Figure 5.6)*. Make sure the potential for improvement is not counterbalanced by a restriction in the air ducting; it should be at least four inches inside diameter, with no sharp bends.

Air-intake tracts of many engines are restricted, which causes performance and fuel-economy losses while operating under heavy throttle. Restriction can be measured with a manifold vacuum gauge *(Figure 5.7)*. The restriction may exist in the cool-air ducting, in the air-cleaner housing, or in both. It's possible to measure the restriction by accelerating or climbing a hill under full throttle at about 3,500 rpm while monitoring vacuum at the intake manifold. Vacuum readings

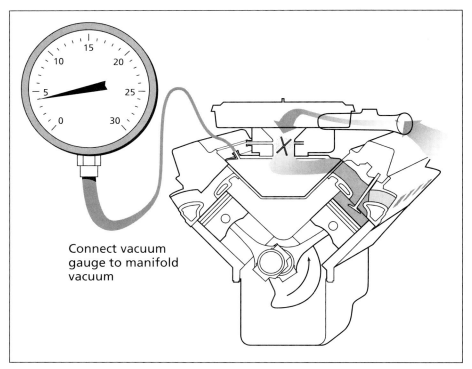

Connect vacuum
gauge to manifold
vacuum

Figure 5.7: A manifold vacuum gauge can be used to measure restriction in an engine's air-intake tract.

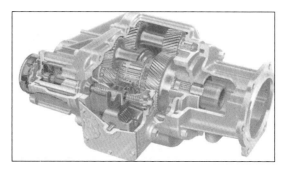

Figure 5.8: Auxiliary transmissions such U.S. Gear (top) and Gear Vendors (bottom) units can be used to add gear versatility for better performance.

should not exceed one to two inches Hg (mercury). Test with the intake system intact, and retest with the cool-air ducting disconnected from the air-cleaner housing to determine the adverse effect of the ducting.

Many air-cleaner housings are inefficient and can be improved, as can the air filters themselves. Effective aftermarket air-induction kits designed specifically for RV engines are available from companies that service the RV industry; their ads usually can be found in RV magazines such as Trailer Life and MotorHome.

While it may seem overly simple, neglect of air filters can cause mileage and performance losses. Restrictions in the air filter will dramatically affect power and fuel mileage; therefore the air-filter element should be inspected every 10,000 miles. Also, look for restrictions in the fresh-air inlet tube. Hoses sometimes collapse, and foreign matter can partially block the inlet. Whether or not the intake tract is modified, the use of a high-performance air-filter can is an effective addition. Typically, these will add several units of horsepower.

Auxiliary Transmissions

Vehicles that are expected to move a lot of weight usually do so with multiple gears. Not so with most RVs, which are limited to four speeds forward. High-line motorhomes are the exception, with 5- or 6-speed transmissions as components of their relatively sophisticated chassis.

Older vehicles with 3-speed automatics are the primary beneficiaries of additional gear ratios, which can be added in the form of auxiliary transmissions. Two primary brands, **U.S. Gear** and **Gear Vendors** *(Figure 5.8)*, are available for installation at many RV repair shops and at the national chain Camping World.

The two units differ in that the U.S. Gear unit can be purchased either as an overdrive or as an underdrive, while the Gear Vendors unit is an overdrive.

In an underpowered vehicle—one, for example, that has a 3.21:1 axle ratio when the load it is towing suggests the need for 3.73:1 gearing—use of the U.S. Gear unit in underdrive mode more than makes up for the difference. The unit's underdrive ratio is 1.25; when applied to a 3.21:1 axle ratio, the effective ratio becomes 4.01:1. Used as an overdrive, the U.S. Gear unit's ratio is 0.80:1.

Use of the Gear Vendors unit (0.78:1 ratio) in a vehicle with a 4.56:1 ratio brings that ratio to an effective 3.55:1 ratio. However, the widespread use of 4-speed overdrive transmissions with 0.7:1 overdrive ratios has reduced the potential fuel-economy benefit of auxiliary overdrive units. It is not effective to run an overdrive ratio on top of another overdrive ratio in most RV situations. Thus the primary benefit of overdrive units is to serve as gear-splitters, providing intermediate gear ranges between first and second and between second and third gears, improving hill-climbability by enabling the driver to keep engine rpm in the best power range.

Camshafts and Valve Gears

Special rocker arms with higher ratios (1.6:1 instead of 1.5:1) have proven to be effective in popular V-8 RV engines. Roller rocker arms and lifters can reduce internal friction substantially, and this can lead to more power and better fuel economy. Roller rocker arms can be added to an existing camshaft but lifters cannot. Since the cam determines how long each valve is open and closed—and the timing in relation to piston movement—a cam change can improve some engines. However, few replacement cams are smog legal. Several companies, including Edelbrock, are expanding their lineup of smog-legal replacement cams in hope of expanding this market.

Cam-replacement is labor-intensive, especially on motorhomes, because the job requires substantial disassembly work. Thus, a cam replacement requires close scrutiny of its advertised results to insure against disappointment.

Computers and Chips

Replacement computers and chips designed to recalibrate electronic fuel-injection systems in gas and diesel engines have created considerable interest among RV owners, and several companies now offer emissions-legal computers or chips that will provide both measurable performance and fuel-economy gains.

The computer chip contains the program that controls air/fuel ratios, spark timing, and the operation of items such as the exhaust-gas recirculation system. Later models also control the automatic transmission shifting. The potential for improvement varies from one vehicle to the next, depending on the design effort devoted to each at the factory. Some vehicles have relatively effective chips while others are in need of improvement. Performance cars usually have stock chips of better design than do light trucks, which means more opportunity for performance and mileage improvement in light trucks. However, look for products designed for heavy-duty operation like trailering and motorhome use. Also, ask if the product requires the use of premium fuel, which adds to the overall cost.

Typically, chips offer around 5 to 15 percent gains in power and from zero to 10 percent more fuel economy. They usually work better when combined with other improvements like a free-flow exhaust system. Aftermarket computer chips are advertised in Trailer Life and MotorHome magazines and can be purchased in many performance shops.

Exhaust Systems

RV engines have varying degrees of restriction in their exhaust manifolds and in other components *(Figure 5.9)*, which has spawned an active aftermarket, producing a variety of smog-legal exhaust systems for tow vehicles as well as motorhomes. All of the RV engines we've tested have benefited substantially from the installation of high-performance aftermarket headers and exhaust systems. Typically, complete systems have yielded up to 15 percent better fuel economy and up to 25 percent more rear-wheel horsepower. Emissions-legal products designed for RV applications should be used for best results. Although some gains can be made with tailpipes and mufflers, the greatest improvements come with well-designed complete exhaust systems including headers, high-flow mufflers, and mandrel-bent pipes.

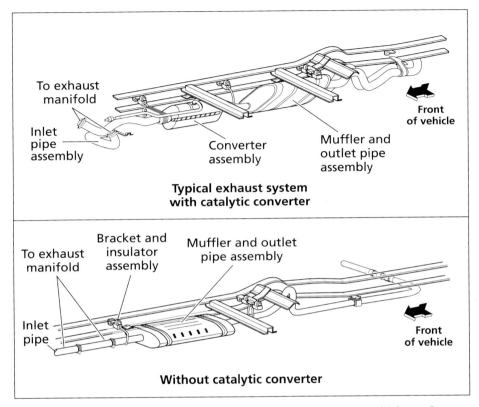

To exhaust manifold

Inlet pipe assembly

Converter assembly

Muffler and outlet pipe assembly

Front of vehicle

Typical exhaust system with catalytic converter

Bracket and insulator assembly

To exhaust manifold

Muffler and outlet pipe assembly

Inlet pipe

Front of vehicle

Without catalytic converter

Figure 5.9: The amount of exhaust restriction varies from one vehicle to the next and can occur at any point from engine to tailpipe.

Exhaust back pressure can be measured at a point downstream from the exhaust manifolds to evaluate the need for exhaust improvements. A fitting must be welded in an exhaust pipe so a pressure gauge can be attached (Figure 5.10). If the system is to remain intact from the converter forward, measure back pressure immediately behind the converter. While accelerating or climbing a grade under full throttle at about 4,000 rpm, exhaust back pressure should not exceed 2 psi.

Catalyst-equipped single-exhaust systems can be converted to a single low-restriction muffler and larger pipes. Excessive back pressure in a noncatalyst vehicle usually can be corrected with dual exhausts with an equalizer pipe and low-restriction mufflers. Again, the pres-

Figure 5.10:
Exhaust
back pres-
sure, an
indicator of
exhaust
restriction,
can be
measured
with a
gauge and
should not
exceed
about 2 psi.

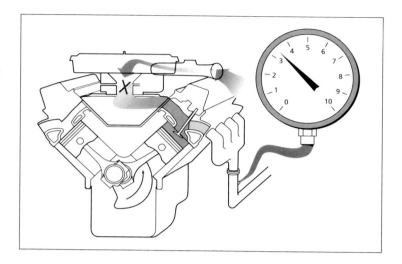

sure gauge will help you determine if changes can be justified. For best results—to go with the substantial improvement of exhaust systems changes—the air-fuel ratio of carbureted engines should be checked on a dynamometer.

Gear Ratios

Sale of vehicles for trailer towing that have improper axle ratios is fairly common even though the motor companies publish guides that suggest engine/axle ratio combinations for specific amounts of trailer weight.

Still a salesman is prone to push vehicles that exist on the sales lot, rather than encouraging the prospective customer to order a vehicle with specific equipment. The result is tow vehicles with axle ratios that may be numerically too high (4.10:1 or 4.56:1, for example) when 3.73:1 may have been adequate, or the opposite, a 3.21:1 axle when 3.73:1 is proper.

When ratios are numerically too high, fuel economy suffers because the engine is turning higher rpm than necessary to move the weight. This is less prevalent with 4-speed automatic transmissions with overdrive top gears. More common is the opposite: numerically low ratios that do not provide enough torque multiplication, which creates inadequate power.

Axle ratios can be changed, although ever-tightening emissions laws have caused most dealerships and many independent shops to decline the business. Off-road vehicle magazines still advertise gearsets and many off-road specialty shops still perform this work on selected vehicles, apparently not including 1997 and later models that are subject to more stringent emissions rules. On-board computers on these vehicles may signal a fault (activating the "check engine" light) if gear ratios or tire diameters are changed.

Ignition

Modifications of a standard electronic-ignition system designed to increase spark output or character don't help RV engines noticeably. The OEM systems are good enough for moderate rpm duty. Manual spark-control units available in performance shops offer the ability to control initial spark advance with a dash-mounted control while on the road. The driver can adjust initial spark timing in response to changing road, fuel, or altitude conditions, which can affect performance and mileage.

The factory-recommended initial spark-advance setting may be somewhat conservative, depending on individual driving conditions, and two additional degrees may add a noticeable measure of throttle response. Factory specifications for spark advance found on stickers affixed under the hood list a specific initial spark-advance number, but factories usually allow variance of plus or minus two degrees. Use the factory setting if the vehicle is prone to spark knock occasionally, which indicates the engine is calibrated as aggressively as possible for the grade of fuel being used.

Retuning

Carbureted engines that were originally tuned for sea-level operation will run rich at high altitudes. If you move from low to high altitude or intend to operate a vehicle for extended periods at high altitude, have the engine tuned for the new operating conditions. This will improve fuel economy and emissions. If you return to low altitudes, have the engine returned to its original setup. The exception to this is vehicles with High Altitude Emission Systems. These vehicles are designed to adapt to varying conditions. This is denoted on an emission-system sticker under the hood on those models.

An engine's tolerance for additional spark advance increases with altitude, which is to say that engines can benefit from more spark advance at high altitude. The reason is that lower atmospheric pressure reduces cylinder pressure. Usually it's inconvenient to change spark-advance settings by readjusting the distributor, but for extended periods of operation at altitude it may be worthwhile. A spark-control system such as the one marketed by MSD, available in automotive-performance shops, allows manual timing control by the driver and is a convenient way to handle it.

Superchargers

Superchargers are bolt-on units that consist of blowers that are belt-driven by the engine's crankshaft to pressurize the intake tract of a gasoline engine, force-feeding more air and fuel than the engine is capable of otherwise ingesting under full throttle. The result is a substantial boost in power, usually accompanied by increased fuel consumption and the need for premium fuel to prevent spark knock (ping).

For the RV owner who seeks the maximum power, the supercharger is the answer. Smog-legal kits are available for GM 5.7- and 7.4-liter engines and Ford 5.0-, 5.8- and 7.5-liter engines. A free-flowing exhaust system is needed for the engine to utilize the full advantage of the supercharger. The manufacturers usually include computer programming to modify fuel delivery, ignition timing, and transmission shift points. Check to make sure the reprogramming is also smog legal.

Turbochargers

Marketed primarily for diesels of 1980s and early 1990s vintage that were naturally aspirated, aftermarket turbochargers are available for the Ford 6.9-liter and early 7.3-liter engines and for the GM 6.2-liter engine. The bolt-on units contain the necessary hardware to reroute the engine's normal air-intake tract through an exhaust-driven blower, creating up to about 9 psi of boost pressure and dramatically increasing engine power output by as much as 60 percent. The turbochargers also tend to reduce maximum exhaust-gas temperatures despite the dramatically increased power output. Purchasers of turbo systems should also invest in a pyrometer (exhaust-gas-temperature gauge) to make sure temperatures do not exceed levels recommended by the turbocharger-kit manufacturer.

Primary manufacturers of the kits are Gale Banks Engineering of Azusa, California, and Advanced Turbo Systems of Murray, Utah.

ON THE ROAD

In an ideal world, we could have maximum fuel mileage and maximum performance at the same time. But we'll have to settle for one or the other. Those of us who want best possible fuel economy must be prepared to make the speed sacrifices necessary to get it. Those who want to maintain a brisk speed must pay the fuel-economy penalty. We may vary between one of these preferences and the other during the same trip.

Cruise control can improve fuel mileage on fairly level roads, especially compared to a driver who is not concentrating on driving for economy. On the other hand, the use of cruise control often reduces mileage in mountainous terrain when we don't think ahead and increase speed a few more miles per hour while descending one hill and facing another. Cruise control also may apply heavy throttle to maintain a set speed, whereas the driver may choose to let speed drop a few miles per hour and use less throttle.

Regardless of your driving style, knowledge of your engine's torque and horsepower curves are helpful in getting what you want. The power curves illustrate an engine's specific output of torque and horsepower. Torque is a twisting force, in this case produced by the engine and measured in pounds-feet. Horsepower is a unit of work over time, calculated by multiplying engine torque by rpm and dividing by 5,252.

An engine is most efficient, doing the maximum amount of work on a given amount of fuel, at its torque peak. Therefore, the most efficient pulling power occurs at or near the engine's torque peak.

When passing another vehicle or climbing a mountain grade, additional power is needed, so we downshift. As the engine speed goes above the torque peak toward the horsepower peak, the amount of force delivered per revolution drops off, but there are more revolutions, so horsepower continues to increase up to a point. Past the horsepower peak, the engine becomes so inefficient at that rpm that the dropoff in torque more than offsets the increase in rpm. The most practical, usable operational range for normal driving is between the torque and horsepower peaks.

A number of power curves are provided here for reference (*Figure 5.11*); if yours is not among them, check with a dealer or call the manufacturer's customer-service hotline.

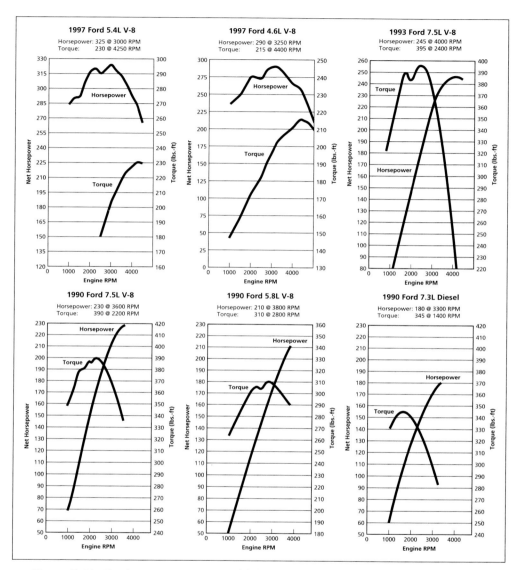

Figure 5.11: Engine power curves published by vehicle manufacturers indicate rpm ranges where best horsepower and torque, measured in pound feet (lb-ft), occur. Curves shown are a sampling from popular engines of the 1980s and 1990s. Acess to 1997 Ford curves was limited.

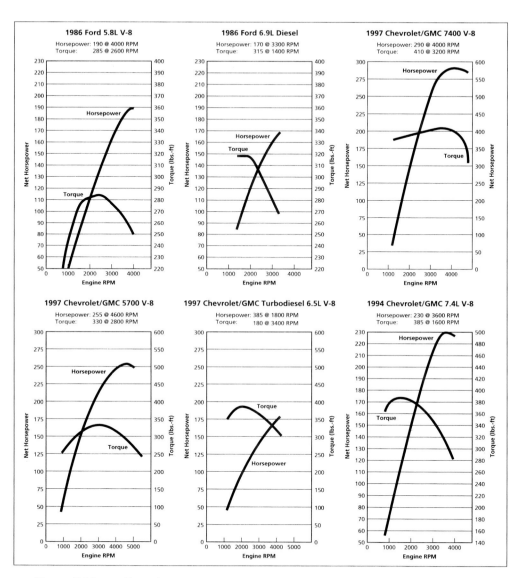

Figure 5.11, *continued*

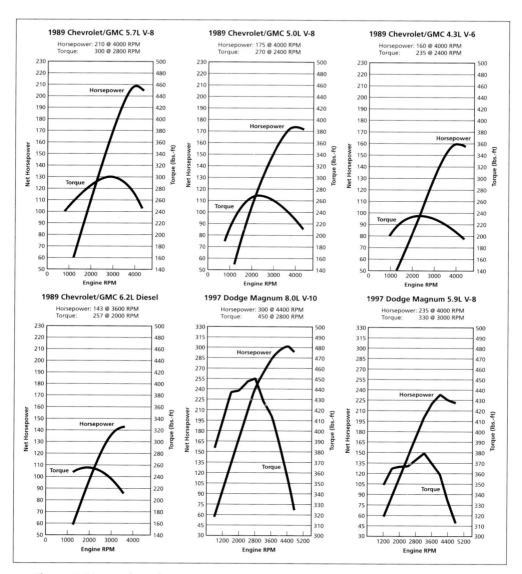

Figure 5.11, *continued*

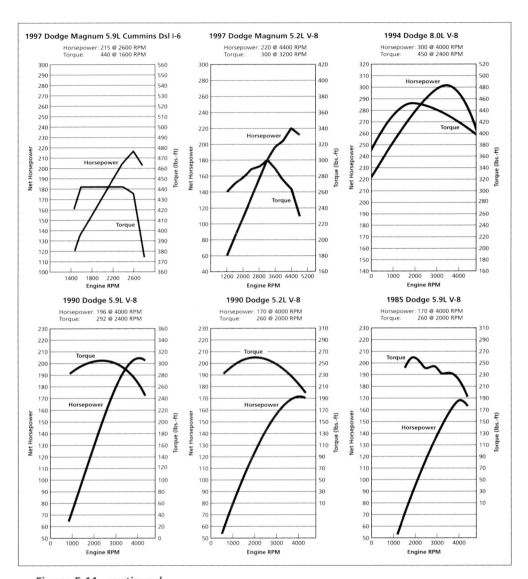

Figure 5.11, *continued*

Fuel Economy

Many factors combined to produce the fuel consumption profile for a specific vehicle, including weight, aerodynamic drag, engine and chassis efficiency, and how the vehicle is driven. The nature of the fuel itself is yet another factor, beyond our control. The introduction of reformulated (oxygenated) gasoline in many areas of the nation in 1995 took a bite out of fuel efficiency, estimated to be 2 to 5 percent. While we can improve all the design factors, making a real difference in any of them can be difficult and costly. We do, however, have immediate control over how the vehicle is driven.

On-the-road rules for best fuel economy are relatively simple:

- Maintain the minimum cruising speed that you find tolerable, creating minimum wind drag.
- Operate in higher gears when possible; avoid downshifting until you're using heavy throttle and cannot maintain your desired minimum speed.
- Accelerate gradually, with minimum pressure on the pedal.
- Maintain constant cruising speeds; varying speeds waste fuel.

Beyond those procedures, your fuel economy will depend on the vehicle type, the chassis equipment selected, and the level of chassis maintenance regularly performed.

HILL CLIMBING AND PASSING

Whether priorities are for fuel economy or performance, knowledge of your engine's power curve is very helpful in putting the engine's power output to its best use. How the accelerator pedal and transmission are handled determine the outcome.

If the transmission is left in drive, its shift program will not allow the engine to over-rev, even under full-throttle operation, although at times it may sound that way. In fact, the programmed transmission upshift point for vehicles with gasoline engines usually is 500 to 1,000 rpm below the engine's redline. Additionally, most current engines with electronic controls will cut power automatically; all diesels are protected by an rpm-limiting governor.

Figure 5.12:
A tachometer
is essential in
operating an
engine at its
highest
potential.

During full-throttle passing we don't always note the speedometer and the automatic upshift point. Thus it's necessary to stage such a maneuver in a nonpassing situation so you can note the upshift speed without a tachometer and calculate engine rpm using the formula included in this chapter. This produces only a rough approximation, because your transmission may shift slightly early or late, rpm-wise. Thus it's better to have a tachometer *(Figure 5.12)*, which will tell you at a glance where you are in the engine's torque and horsepower ranges.

During your full-throttle test run, note the vehicle's ability to gain speed. It might be strong throughout the entire rpm range, or it may seem to diminish before it reaches the upshift point. If the engine upshifts before 4,000 rpm, the transmission programming probably is not working properly, even if you either have an engine with an unusually low-horsepower peak (Ford 7.5-liter engine of late 1980s/ early 1990s vintage, for example).

If the transmission upshifts sooner than 4,000 rpm, shift to second gear and perform another run, noting rpm or road speed and releasing the throttle when you notice that the rate of acceleration has begun to diminish. This will identify your "best power" point. If you have noted the road speed, you can calculate the rpm in second gear at that speed.

When climbing grades, there are a couple of different approaches you can use:

1. *Conservative.* Allow road speed to drop until the engine is in its peak torque range. That will be a narrow range for some gasoline engines—200 to 300 rpm—and a rather broad one for some others and for most diesels. For example, the torque peak of late-model Ford 460s occurs at 2,200 rpm and drops off sharply above and below that level. If your road speed at 2,200 rpm is satisfactory, hold at that level because it is the most efficient use of engine power.

   If your engine is a Dodge 8-liter V-10, the power curve tells you that the range of substantial torque output is rather broad, extending from about 1,800 to 2,700 rpm. You may want to allow rpm to drop to about 2,000 rpm before downshifting.

   However, if it appears that the grade is steep enough that you will not be able to avoid dropping below the peak torque rpm, downshift before you reach that point or the loss of vehicle momentum will carry you below the peak torque rpm, requiring a downshift to an even lower gear.

2. *Performance-oriented.* This approach involves downshifting at what-ever road speed that will raise engine rpm to your previously estab-lished "best power" point or slightly above. Downshifting a gasoline engine from third to second at 3,000 rpm will raise rpm to about 4,000. This allows the driver to maintain the best possible vehicle momentum and have the option of backing off a bit for a slightly slower pace, less engine noise and better fuel economy.

Maximum rpm

If your "best power" rpm level seems too high, it isn't, assuming the engine is being cooled properly. When necessary, all popular engines used in RVs can be operated up to their redlines, which usually are a few hundred rpm above their rated peak horsepower rpm points, to get maximum performance. In fact, the engines are tested at full throt-tle at peak horsepower rpm for extended periods to determine dura-bility. Marine conversions of the GM 7.4-liter engine, for example, are rated to run continuously at full throttle in their peak horsepower range, 4,200 to 4,600 rpm. Magnum versions of the 7.4-liter engine are rated to run at full power up to 5,000 rpm.

Many external components are installed for marine use, but the internal balance of the engine and the strength of its block and reciprocating parts are not altered. Thus these engines are virtually identical to their counterparts in light trucks and motorhomes from the standpoint of suitability for high-rpm operation—assuming that engine operating temperature is not excessive.

Diesel engines are tightly controlled by governor mechanisms, which simplifies the performance equation if automatic transmission shift points are set properly. The following simple tests will determine if they are:

Test 1: Shift to second gear and accelerate under full throttle from about 40 MPH until the governor limits rpm. Note the rpm level.

Test 2: Shift to third gear, begin at 40 MPH, and floor the accelerator, allowing the transmission to upshift automatically. If the transmission upshifts at or about the rpm level noted in Test 1, transmission programming is correct. If it upshifts early, you can get better uphill and passing performance from your diesel by manually controlling the upshift point to coincide with the governed rpm.

Operating any engine under heavy throttle at high rpm assumes that engine-coolant temperature does not rise beyond about 225°F and that spark knock (gasoline models) does not occur. It also assumes that the owner is using top-quality oil and changing it at proper intervals.

Calculating rpm Versus Road Speed

Engine rpm can be calculated for various road speeds. This is very useful for predicting the effect of different gear ratios or tire sizes before purchase:

$$rpm = \frac{R \times M \times MPH}{60}$$

R= Transmission gear ratio multiplied by axle ratio.*
M= Tire revolutions per mile (see Chapter 2) for a method of calculating this factor)
MPH= Road speed
60= A constant

*Note that most overdrive transmissions have a direct gear ratio (1:1) in third gear; top (O/D) gear is around 0.70:1.

A list of engine rpm/road speed figures can also be posted near, but not obstructing, the driver's field of vision if you don't have a tachometer.

Vacuum Versus Manifold Absolute Pressure

Most of us have encountered a manifold vacuum gauge that's marked in inches of mercury (in.-hg.). These gauges start with normal atmospheric pressure (29.92 in.-hg.) being counted as zero, and as pressure decreases below normal atmospheric it indicates the change as an increase in vacuum.

Vacuum readings decrease when altitude increases at the rate of about 1 in-.hg. per 1,000 feet of change in elevation. The gauge readings still are valid relative to the operation of a carburetor's fuel-enrichment system, but when driving in high altitudes, it's difficult or impossible to maintain high vacuum readings.

Differential pressure at the venturis is what makes carburetors work, and measurement of manifold vacuum is a useful indicator. However, with the advent of fuel injection, especially with supercharging and turbocharging, another system of measurement was needed—manifold absolute pressure (MAP). This type of measurement was used for years in aircraft.

With MAP, all readings begin at zero, which really is absolute zero—total vacuum. Any increase in pressure gives a positive pressure reading.

In a naturally aspirated (nonturbo or nonsupercharged) engine at full throttle, the air pressure in the intake manifold will be almost the same as the outside air (29.92 in.-hg.). Vacuum gauges only sense the difference between the ambient air pressure and the pressure in the manifold. For example, with a vacuum gauge, full throttle at sea level might yield 0 in.-hg., but with MAP, it would read 29.92 in.-hg. At full throttle at high altitude, MAP might be 20 in.-hg. but the vacuum gauge would still read 0.

Air/Fuel Ratio Monitors (Gasoline Engines Only)

Several aftermarket manufacturers now offer air/fuel ratio monitors. These units generally employ an automotive oxygen sensor mounted in the exhaust and a small microprocessor that illuminates light-emitting diodes (LEDs) on a monitor panel. The LEDs indicate what the air/fuel ratio is at the moment. This allows the driver to know if the engine is getting the proper fuel mixture and at what point fuel enrichment occurs.

Air/fuel ratios of engines at normal operating temperature typically range between about 11.5:1 under full load to slightly higher than 15:1 during light throttle and coast conditions. A ratio of 14.7:1 during part throttle cruise is considered ideal for low emissions and good fuel economy.

Monitoring air/fuel ratios can be especially helpful with the reformulated fuels now on the market. If an engine is getting too much fuel (too rich) it will waste gas, develop carbon deposits, and may ruin the catalytic converter (if so equipped). If an engine is not getting enough fuel (too lean), it may backfire, surge, or stumble, and eventually may burn valves and pistons.

Boost-Pressure Gauges
(Turbocharged and Supercharged Engines Only)

A boost gauge is a welcome addition to engines with pressurized intakes. These instruments generally measure intake manifold pressure in psi (metric gauges use Bar; one Bar equals about 15 psi). Boost gauges allow the driver to monitor the output and effectiveness of the turbocharger or supercharger. Some diesels also don't have an automatic wastegate to limit pressure; with a gauge the driver can limit boost by varying the accelerator. By avoiding excessive boost, a driver can reduce stress on the engine.

Exhaust-Gas-Temperature Gauges (Diesels Only)

Exhaust-gas-temperature gauges (EGTs) monitor the heat present in the exhaust gases. This temperature varies directly with load and is a good indicator of how hard a diesel engine is being "worked." At idle, exhaust temperatures of diesel engines are typically around 300° F. Under full load, temperatures can soar to well over 1,300° F.

Most diesel-engine manufacturers recommend that peak EGT should not exceed about 1,200° F; check and follow the recommendation for your engine. If EGT approaches this maximum, ease off the accelerator enough to stay below the redline temperature to insure engine durability and long service life.

Manifold Vacuum Gauges (Gasoline Engines Only)

Manifold vacuum gauges are useful tools for driving more efficiently and for monitoring the operational status of the engine *(Figure 5.13)*. The gauge is connected to the intake passages of a gasoline engine by a small hose so it can monitor the varying levels of pressure (partial vacuum) inside the manifold. These levels change in relation to throttle position and load. By positioning the gauge where it's easy to see, the driver has a constant reminder of throttle position and is prone to drive with a steadier and lighter foot on the accelerator pedal.

Electronic fuel-injection systems gradually enrich fuel mixtures in response to heavier throttle so there is no single transition point (indicated in vacuum-gauge readings) where a significant change occurs. Electronic fuel-injection systems gradually enrich mixtures by increasing the dwell period (time during which the injector is spraying fuel into the engine).

However, there is a definite important enrichment point with carburetors. All carburetors have fuel-enrichment systems that allow lean mixtures to be used for light- to medium-throttle conditions and richer mixtures for heavy throttle. Four-barrel carburetors have three such systems: cruise, primary power, and secondary power. Two-barrel carburetors have two: cruise and power.

The four-barrel carburetor of an engine propelling an RV on relatively level highways in low altitude (below about 5,000 feet) operates in the cruise range at light to medium throttle, producing vacuum readings between eight and twelve inches. The readings are affected by such things as the weight of the vehicle, efficiency of the engine, and effective gear ratios.

When moderate hills are encountered, vacuum readings may drop into the four- to eight-inch range. Therein lies the opportunity for fuel-economy improvement. The transition in most carburetors between the cruise fuel-metering system and the primary power-enrichment system occurs at six to seven inches of manifold vacuum, and with some carburetors, it may occur as low as four to

Figure 5.13: Manifold vacuum gauge indicates throttle usage and is helpful in driving for best possible fuel economy.

five inches. It's possible for the driver to maintain vacuum readings above six inches rather than slightly below that level for significant fuel-economy improvement.

Although it might follow logically that downshifting early to maintain vacuum levels above six inches would also improve fuel consumption, that's not entirely true because the engine uses additional fuel at higher rpm. It's simply best to hold vacuum above about six inches as long as possible, then use heavier throttle until vehicle speed drops to a comfortable downshift point.

The secondary metering system of a carburetor further enriches air-fuel ratios, but the vacuum gauge is less useful in monitoring its action, which occurs near full throttle.

The vacuum gauge will not single out any particular transition point in fuel metering. However, it's useful as a reminder of throttle position.

It's important to establish reasonable goals and make changes that are designed to work together. For RV use, it's more important to increase low- and mid-range torque and horsepower than to sacrifice that to gain power at high rpm. Improvements in performance and fuel economy can be elusive, but with a well-thought-out plan, it should be possible to make noticeable gains.

Making a Vehicle Last Longer

In this chapter the following items will be covered:

- Developing Proper Vehicle Startup and Driving Habits
- Engine Cooling
- Engine Oils and Oil Additives
- Automatic Transmission Fluids
- Manual Transmission Oil
- Detonation and Preignition
- Cooldown
- Reformulated Gasoline
- Engine-Service Intervals
- Effects of Storage
- Diesel Engines
- On the Road with Diesels

Vehicles, being rather complex assemblages of parts that work in close tolerances, have the unfortunate tendency to wear out. Indeed, the only thing that keeps many of their parts from wearing out posthaste is a microscopically thin film of oil or grease that separates the metal parts and carries heat away.

The engine is the most expensive single vehicle component and usually require the most maintenance. It isn't uncommon that some engines give outrageously good service, while others are quite mediocre. Although the original design and quality of the engine are major factors in longevity, the owner can get the long-term durability—extended life of any engine—by using the wide variety of techniques listed in this chapter.

DEVELOPING PROPER VEHICLE STARTUP AND DRIVING HABITS

Even engines of the highest quality can be adversely affected by poor driving habits. A common bad habit is a tendency to start the engine, rev it a couple of times, drop the transmission into gear, and roar away. An engine needs a few seconds for oil to get into full circulation, particularly to the valve train, which is the last to see oil flow. When the engine is revved right after starting, the valve train, as well as other surfaces, may be marginally lubricated *(Figure 6.1)*. Engine oil is supposed to prevent metal-to-metal contact, but cold starts are a particularly vulnerable time. Revving the engine creates more metal-to-metal contact during this period, and thousands of cold starts accumulate to cause serious wear.

Similarly, revving the engine just as it's shut off causes unneeded wear and stress. Turbodiesel drivers should also allow their engines to idle for several minutes after a hard run before shutdown to allow the turbocharger to cool down. This helps prevent "cooking" of the oil in the turbo and saves the bearings.

The type of driving we do usually cannot be altered significantly, but it's interesting to note that city driving is estimated to be about 17 percent less efficient than steady highway cruising; short trips of three miles or less increase fuel consumption due to the fact that the engine has not had time to fully come up to normal operating temperature.

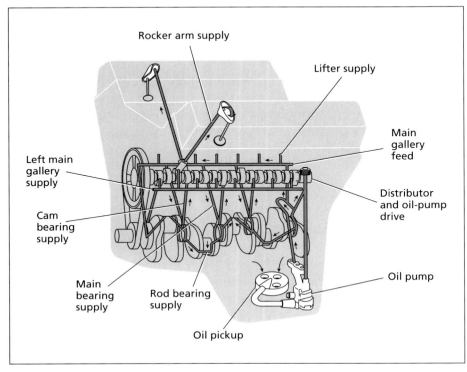

Figure 6.1: Oil flows under pressure to lubricate all of the engine's moving parts. The valve train is the last item in the system to receive lubrication after a cold start.

Cold Starts

When starting a fuel-injected engine, it's not necessary to touch the accelerator pedal. Without touching the pedal, engine rpm will rise to a preset fast-idle level that is best for initial oil circulation.

The proper method of cold-starting a carbureted engine is to depress the accelerator pedal about halfway to set the choke, and release the pedal. This will result in a fast idle (about 1,000 rpm) when the engine starts. Giving the engine too much throttle while cranking usually will result in initial revving to 2,000 rpm or higher, which is hard on the marginally lubricated parts of a cold engine.

To properly cold-start diesel engines, turn on the ignition and wait until the preheater or glow-plug timer light indicates it's okay to start the engine. Do not pump the throttle. If the engine doesn't start within about ten seconds, turn the ignition off and on again to recycle the cold-starting device. Allow the starter to cool after prolonged cranking.

Regardless of the type of fuel system or engine, when cold-starting an engine, run it at a fast idle for about twenty seconds, allowing oil to circulate to the most remote sections of the engine (such as the valve train), before placing the transmission in gear. This small delay will assure good oil circulation. Keep engine rpm low and avoid heavy acceleration until the engine has reached its normal operating temperature.

Extended idling of the engine during warmup is not a good practice because fuel vaporization is poor and cylinder pressures are relatively low. Warmup occurs more rapidly if the vehicle is driven soon after being started.

Stop-and-go driving creates many more opportunities for wear, especially in cold weather when fuel enrichment occurs with each restart. This kind of driving is known to be hardest on engines. The driving situation that creates the least engine wear is light-load cruising. RV driving undoubtedly qualifies somewhere in between these two extremes, at least in moderate weather. When weather is hot, RV trips can produce high engine-oil temperatures and an increased tendency for gasoline engines to spark knock (ping or detonate). RVing typically is classified by motor companies as heavy-duty service, requiring accelerated engine-oil change intervals.

Cylinder Washdown

A significant cause of accelerated wear of gasoline engines during cold starts is gasoline—too much of it. On carbureted engines, chokes produce rich fuel mixtures; raw gasoline then floods into cylinders and washes the microscopically thin film of oil from the cylinder walls. However, all liquid fuel engines do this to some extent. This allows metal-to-metal contact between piston rings and cylinder walls. Cylinder washdown can cause accelerated piston ring and cylinder wear, leading to the loss of the ring seal, the reduction of compression, and excessive oil consumption.

During a cold start, the engine should not backfire, stall, or stumble. If it does, readjust the choke or (choke pulloff) to a richer setting, saving fuel as well as piston rings. On the other hand, if the engine chugs or produces black smoke from the tailpipe, lean the choke adjustments.

On fuel-injected gasoline-powered vehicles, cold-start enrichment circuits are more accurate and normally do not cause too much enrichment.

With any system, waiting about twenty seconds for oil to circulate and avoiding heavy acceleration until the temperature is up are important.

Another fairly uncommon but very serious cause of cylinder washdown in carbureted engines is fuel percolation after hot shutdown. Also, if the carburetor-float level is too high, the engine is very hot, or the fuel-inlet valve tends to leak, fuel may drip into the intake manifold after the engine is shut off. This washes oil from the cylinders and causes partial flooding that requires excessive cranking to restart the engine. Cranking the engine under this condition causes rapid wear of piston rings.

Avoid extended engine idling, during which fuel vaporization and combustion temperatures are not ideal. The result is less lubrication and a higher level of cylinder washdown, causing accelerated wear, as well as an increase in carbon deposits.

On the Road

Most engines are designed to be operated for short periods at speeds slightly beyond their peak horsepower rpm, such as in passing situations when the accelerator pedal is "floored" and the transmission downshifts. Horsepower/torque graphs featured on pages 62–64 identify peak horsepower rpm for various engines. For example, the Chevrolet/GMC Vortec 7400 engine's peak horsepower occurs at 4,200 rpm. This represents the 7.4-liter engine's upper limit for best performance while passing other vehicles or hill-climbing when maximum performance and speed are desired. Engine rpm levels above 4,000 may seem high for V-8 engines, but in fact engineers say the engines can be operated even above the peak horsepower rpm if the driver needs to extend the operational range for maximum speed in lower gears for short periods of time. The engine redline for the Vortec 7400, for example, is 4,800 rpm.

A complicating factor in operating an engine under heavy throttle at any rpm, but especially at high rpm, is heat. Engine-coolant operating temperature may climb to 230°F or higher, and engine-oil temperature may approach or exceed 300°F, depending on the engine's and vehicle's design and mechanical condition. Heat also raises the engine's fuel-octane requirements, leading to another serious factor, detonation (engine ping), which can quickly damage engines. Thus, heat may bring an engine into a crisis situation that might be repeated several times a day.

Barring an increase in operating temperature beyond the upper end of the normal operating range (about 225°F), engines that are in good condition can be operated continuously under heavy throttle at their peak horsepower rpm. More conservative owners may want to limit rpm to 80 percent of peak horsepower rpm.

ENGINE COOLING

The need for adequate engine cooling cannot be overemphasized, despite the fact that engine metallurgy and oils have been greatly improved during the past decade to withstand more heat. In the 1970s, it was not uncommon for heat to cause oils to thicken, due to oxidation, into something resembling hot asphalt that would not drain from the crankcase. Good-quality oils (identified by the American Petroleum Institute starburst symbol) are much better now, but quality may still vary. High temperatures create tremendous heat loads on lubricants, which may reduce their ability to prevent metal-to-metal contact. It's wise to make sure cooling systems are in the best possible condition and that engine temperature gauges are accurate.

Cooling systems of late-model vehicles are usually able to restrain temperature rise under severe operating conditions. Most systems keep engine-coolant temperatures from exceeding about 230°F through use of viscous-clutch fans designed to go into high-speed modes when temperatures reach 215°F to 225°F. The fans freewheel until engine temperature reaches a certain point, and then the fan clutches more fully engage, raising fan rpm for maximum airflow.

An engine that tends to incur a noticeable temperature rise (possibly accompanied by a tendency to spark knock) needs help. It may require additional cooling capacity such as a thicker radiator, a slight reduction in initial spark timing, higher octane gasoline to prevent

Figure 6.2: Proper engine cooling depends on the correct operation of the viscous-drive fan clutch which is belt-driven by the engine.

spark knock, or something as simple as unclogging the exhaust gas recirculation (EGR) passages.

Late-model engines are designed to operate at relatively high temperatures, 195°F to 205°F, to help vaporize fuel and reduce emissions. These temperature levels are intended to control emissions and to contribute to better fuel economy. The thermostat is regarded as a component of the emissions-control system, which means that it is covered by general prohibitions against tampering.

On the opposite end of the spectrum, running an engine too cool can cause accelerated wear and increased combustion deposits inside the engine. General Motors estimates that cylinder wear increases eightfold with coolant temperature at 100°F compared with the normal 195°F. Thermostats sometimes stick in the open position, evidenced by gauge readings that do not rise to normal except in hot weather or under heavy load.

The ingredients of a healthy cooling system include:

- Radiator of adequate size, maintained properly
- 50–50 mix of antifreeze and distilled water, changed every two years unless extended-life coolant is used
- Engine fan of adequate size that goes into high-rpm mode (makes more noise) when engine temperature rises to around 225°F to 230°F
- Effective fan shroud
- Unrestricted airflow through radiator

Inoperative fan clutches are a common cause of excessive operating temperatures. When engine-coolant temperature exceeds 210° to 230°(calibration differs according to type of engine), the fan should go into its high-speed mode, dramatically increasing airflow through the radiator.

Most cooling systems designed for 14 to 17 psi of pressure will not boil out (release pressure from the radiator cap) until the temperature reaches approximately 260°F to 270°F. But that's far too hot if you expect the engine to live very long. Peak operating temperature even under very high ambient conditions should not exceed 230°F, and even that is high enough to push many engines to spark knock. A coolant temperature of 230°F is the highest point at which the engine fan should go into its high-speed mode to arrest temperature rise. When the fan locks in, a higher level of fan noise should be audible. If it isn't, and if temperature climbs steadily, the fan clutch *(Figure 6.2)* may be in need of replacement.

When antifreeze is added, it should be mixed with distilled water rather than tap water. The reason is that tap water contains minerals. When the water is heated in the cooling system, the minerals deposit on the surfaces of the cooling system, particularly on water passages inside the cylinder heads and the radiator. Thus, the engine gradually builds up a coating of mineral deposits that retards the transfer of heat into the coolant, increasing combustion-chamber temperature and the tendency of the engine to detonate.

It's important that cooling-system maintenance never be neglected because the effects are difficult or nearly impossible to reverse. Certainly, the radiator can be reconditioned, but deposits and corrosion inside of the block usually are permanent.

TIPS THAT WORK

Fancy Fan

If you're the owner of a tow vehicle, you are probably treated to high engine temperatures and more engine-fan noise than you'd like whenever the going gets tough. This is usually the result of the thermostatically controlled engine-fan clutch engaging whenever it senses increased cooling needs. In hot climates, the roar may never subside—making it a constant irritation to vehicle occupants.

Fortunately, there is a solution. You need only equip your tow vehicle with a couple of the new-generation, high-volume, electric radiator fans. These are easily attached to a vehicle's radiator core, and are readily available from most automotive outlets and many performance-oriented mail-order houses. However, make certain that you purchase only high-capacity electric fans designed for applications of this type.

Once installed, the fans can be wired to operate manually through a dash-mounted switch, or to activate automatically through a temperature sensor, or both. I suggest the latter, since it gives the driver greater control over engine cooling, especially in traffic.

The fans can also be set so that one comes on at a lower temperature than the other. Whenever a slow-up occurs, the fans can be turned on in anticipation of an engine temperature rise. A thermostat in the circuit is advantageous because cooling will start when needed, even if the driver forgets to flip the switch.

Additionally, the extra drag produced by a continuously engaged, high-capacity, steel fan will noticeably reduce overall fuel economy. And, because conventional fans

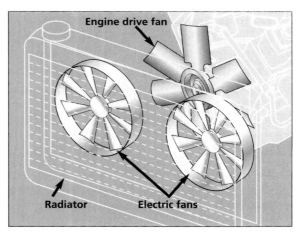

and thermostatic hubs are bolted to the water-pump shaft, the supporting bearing often gets quite a workout. This can result in premature failure, particularly if the fan itself is even slightly out of balance. With this change, the original engine-driven fan can sometimes be removed altogether, since it may no longer be needed in the presence of two high-output electric models. This will give the water-pump bearing a break, and allow the engine to produce more power with greater efficiency.

Richard Mater, Santa Maria, California

ENGINE OILS AND OIL ADDITIVES

The search for the best engine oils has led in many different directions and has been under way for about as long as vehicles have occupied America's roadways. Advertising claims ballyhoo one brand against another. The consumer's only accurate guide, other than long personal experience with a particular brand and grade, are the ratings by the American Petroleum Institute (API) for quality and performance. Two symbols indicate the rating, an API service symbol, which includes the viscosity rating *(Figure 6.3)*, and a starburst symbol, which indicates the type of use *(Figure 6.4)*. Both symbols insure the oil has passed API's performance tests, and are displayed on the container.

Figure 6.3:
The API service symbol indicates viscosity and grade of oil, which must match recommendations of the vehicle manufacturer.

Current Engine-Oil Ratings

The following are the current ratings for engine-oils:

- SJ for gasoline engines in cars, vans, and light trucks
- SH for gasoline engines in cars, vans, and light trucks This category is no longer valid inside API's service symbol after August, 1997, except in combination with certain C categories.
- CG-4 for high-speed four-stroke diesel engines
- CF-4 for high-performance four-stroke and turbocharged diesel engines
- CF-2 for two-stroke diesel engines
- CE and CD ratings for diesel engines were discontinued after 1995

Figure 6.4:
The starburst symbol indicates gasoline-engine usage and energy conservation capability.

WHAT A MULTI-VISCOSITY OIL INCLUDES

A multi-viscosity additive package includes the following:

- **Pour-point Depressants:** Straight mineral oils tend to congeal into waxlike consistency in low temperatures. Special additives keep the oil molecules from joining, thereby keeping the oil liquid.

- **Oxidation and Bearing-Corrosion Inhibitors:** These compounds are designed to slow the rate of oxidation and to provide a coating for bearings.

- **Rust and Corrosion Inhibitors:** Water-laden air enters engine crankcases, and the water condenses when the engine cools. It mixes with the oil and causes formation of acids. Additives are needed to neutralize the acids and help coat metal surfaces to keep acids from attacking them.

- **Detergent/Dispersant Additives:** Combustion byproducts must be kept in suspension so they can be drained out with the oil. It's important to note that these additives will not clean sludge and varnish out of an engine; their primary role is to prevent sludge formation. The role of these additives is one of the reasons new oil tends to darken soon after an oil change. As these additives are used up, they perform their function, which is why the oil must be changed.

- **Foam Inhibitors:** Oil is subjected to high pressure and engine components that are rotating at high speeds, so it mixes and becomes aerated. Because aerated oil does not work very well, these inhibitors, mainly silicones, are used to reduce foaming.

- **Viscosity:** Oil viscosity (thickness) changes with temperature, and since many engines are operated in widely varying temperatures, oils that maintain fairly consistent viscosity can provide good circulation during cold starts, while also affording proper lubrication under high temperatures. Polymers are used to provide this versatility in multigrade petroleum-based oils. For example, SAE 10W-30 is listed by many motor companies as suitable for use in an ambient temperature range from 0°F to an excess of 100°F, while SAE 30 is listed as suitable for a range of 40°F to in excess of 100°F.

- **Extreme-Pressure Additives:** Certain chemicals that tend to be attracted to metal surfaces are known as boundary lubricants. They help prevent metals from galling or from welding to each other under high temperatures when the oil film is very thin, such as in the cam-to-lifter contact area.

Multigrade oils include a complex package of additives designed to extend suitability for operation in widely varying temperatures as well as other performance functions *(see page 132 for a description of additives)*.

In order for an oil to qualify for the highest rating, it must pass a series of performance tests. Each test is used to evaluate a specific characteristic of oil, such as protection against wear, corrosion rust, and oxidation due to heat. For example, an oxidation/wear test is conducted for sixty-four hours with the oil at 300°F to measure the oil's tendency to permit excessive wear and to measure thickening, sludge, and varnish formation. Resistance to these deteriorating factors are important aspects of the classification. All SH and SJ oils are assumed to have passed the 300°F test.

Selecting Oil Grades

Automotive companies universally specify multigrades in owner's manuals, and most no longer list single grades such as SAE 30, which was the preferred oil for GM's 7.4-liter engine in the company's motorhome chassis for many years, as suitable.

Owner's manuals for the Chevrolet and Ford motorhome chassis and light trucks list 5W-30 as preferred for gasoline engines in all temperatures and 10W-30 as suitable for temperatures above 0°F.

Chevrolet specifies SAE 15W-40 down to 0°F for diesel engines and 10W-30 from 32°F. to sub-zero temperatures. SAE 30 oil is listed as acceptable for diesels above 32°F, which is the only mention of SAE 30 in manufacturer literature on gasoline engines. Only Chevrolet even lists SAE 30 as acceptable (above 32°F) for the 6.5-liter turbodiesel, but specifies the preferred oil grade as SAE 15W-40 for the naturally aspirated diesel. GM specifically recommends against SAE 20W-50 "or any other grade" not listed in its recommendations for gasoline and diesel engines. Engineers suggest that the viscosity spread of SAE 20W-50 is too great, requiring too many additives. Many years ago GM advised against use of SAE 10W-40 for the same reasons, although other motor companies continued to approve the grade.

Federal fuel-economy regulations also motivate manufacturers to recommend relatively low-viscosity multigrades. Also, there is the possibility that the vehicle owner who uses a heavier oil may neglect to change to a lighter oil for cold-weather driving. Single-grade oils such as SAE 30 do not circulate well immediately after a cold-engine startup in temperatures below 40°F, creating the possibility of accelerated wear. Single-grade oils create additional resistance to movements of engine components under all conditions, compared to multigrades with lower reference numbers. These companies apparently do not believe most motorists are conscientious enough to avoid misusing single-grade oils.

In support of the recommendations, engineers admit that they are motivated by fuel-economy considerations in vehicles under 8,500 pounds GVWR, but add that they are convinced the latest lightweight multigrades carrying the starburst symbol will protect engines under extreme operating situations. One veteran engine-design manager admitted he had always favored thicker oils for hot-weather situations but was won over by his own engine durability testing with the lower viscosity oils.

Synthetic Oils

Most manufacturers, including Mobil, recommend following the vehicle manufacturer's oil-change intervals, since additive packages in all oils are neutralized by the combustion byproducts that form inside an engine.

Few engine manufacturers specifically recommend synthetics, although they are included in lists of approved oils if they carry the latest ratings—and providing the vehicle manufacturer's oil-change intervals are observed. General Motors has used Mobil 1 synthetic oil as the factory fill for the Corvette LT-1 and LT-5 engines.

Modern synthetics may be mixed with conventional oils, although it dilutes the properties of the synthetic. Motor companies insist that regular oil changes are mandatory for engine durability because contaminants that are absorbed by the oil must be flushed from the engine. Good synthetics are generally recognized as having higher performance levels than petroleum-based oils because of the following:

- High-temperature stability
- Cold-temperature performance
- Improved protection against engine deposits

Among these attributes, better tolerance for high temperatures may be a primary advantage for RV owners because their engines pull heavy loads under sustained heavy throttle and high engine rpm, often during hot weather. Although the heat resistance of conventional oils has been improved steadily during the past few years, true synthetics still apparently have a definite edge. They resist oxidation, which means high resistance to varnish formation and thickening.

Some oils are a blend of synthetic and conventional oils. The oil's characteristics will depend on the percentage of each type plus the quality of the base stocks. Blends may not have the same capability to protect at high-temperature as true synthetics.

The base compounds used for synthetic oils vary among brands. Most synthetics use polyalphaolefins and esters for the base stock, combined with an additive package. The molecules are of consistent size and shape while molecules of conventional mineral oils vary widely in size and shape. They tend to clump together and thicken at cold temperatures. Under high temperatures, the smaller molecules tend to boil off, thickening the oil.

TIPS THAT WORK

Arresting Thought

On my last RV trip, I stopped at a rest stop for a break. As I was getting ready to leave near dusk, I decided to do a quick underhood fluid check. As luck would have it, I dropped the oil-filler opening cap. After spending about 20 minutes looking for it in the approaching darkness, I decided to make sure that this event did not happen again.

I stopped at a hardware store in the next town and bought a 24-inch length of small-loop chain. Then, with a small washer and a sheet-metal screw, I attached the chain to the top of the cap (a rubber push-in type). I used a plastic wire bundle tie to secure the other end of the chain to a group of wires near the top of the firewall, leaving a little slack to allow for engine movement. No more lost oil caps for me.

Jack Ewald, West Union, Ohio

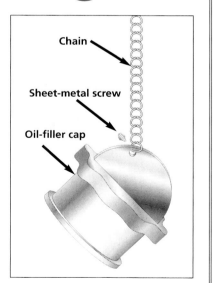

Chain

Sheet-metal screw

Oil-filler cap

Energy-Conserving Oils

Oils that are categorized as energy conserving carry the starburst symbol. The designation is carried by most popular 5W-30 and 10W-30 oils.

Use of oils with the starburst label, indicating energy conservation, are estimated to improve fuel economy by 2.7 percent or greater. These estimates apparently refer to passenger-car driving; less improvement may occur in heavily loaded engines in severe service.

Oil Additives

With the complex package of additives present in modern oils, no additional ones are needed—despite the advertising claims for a broad variety of oil additives. Some additives are merely viscosity improvers and others claim to reduce friction. Engineers at the motor companies consistently maintain that modern oils have all the additives they need and that additional additives serve no useful purpose. Indeed, in some cases, additives are said to seriously degrade the oil's performance. Manufacturers of aftermarket oil-improver products usually are not able to provide authoritative analyses by independent testing laboratories to back up their claims of reduced engine wear.

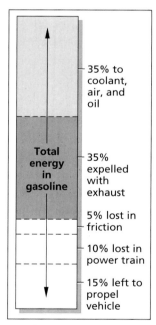

Figure 6.5:
The engine oil must absorb up to 20 percent of the engine's heat output.

Oil Cooling

Any oil can benefit by operating under reasonable temperatures. An oil film only 0.001-inch thick must lubricate, seal, and cool engine components in areas where combustion temperatures range from 2,000°F to 3,000°F. The oil must soak up as much as 20 percent of the engine's heat output *(Figure 6.5)*. While the coolant mixture circulating through the engine's water jacket cools the upper part of the engine (including cylinder heads, cylinders, and valves) the oil must cool the crankshaft and connecting-rod bearings, the camshaft and its bearings, the timing gears, the pistons, and other components.

In racing situations, coolers are used to keep temperatures in the low 200s, helping engine components withstand extreme high rpm levels under full-throttle conditions.

In contrast, oil temperatures in RV engines usually run 250°F to 270°F during summertime driving and may exceed 300°F on grades in hot weather. Modern oils are designed to resist breakdown at high temperatures, but the fact that oil in many RVs will approach 300°F under hot-weather hill-climbing conditions provides a severe test for an oil's ability to resist breakdown. Engine manufacturers say that temperatures up to 285°F are within their design parameters.

Oil cooling has obvious benefits for RV engines, but the vehicle owner must weigh the cost of adding an oil cooler against the amount of driving that will be done under hot-weather conditions. Owners who frequently drive mountainous terrain in hot weather and routinely see temperatures that exceed 275°F (in the sump) are prime candidates for additional oil cooling. Oil coolers that are suitable for most RV engines are available at performance-equipment stores and RV supply stores.

AUTOMATIC TRANSMISSION FLUIDS

Automatic transmission fluid operating temperatures measured in the sump should be kept between 135°F and 250°F (the temperature in the output line to the heat exchanger will be higher). To keep peak temperatures from exceeding 250°F, the normal operating temperature should not exceed 225°F. Transmission fluid is not changed as often as is engine oil, and it has more time to oxidize, hence the lower suggested temperature maximums.

Even with proper cooling, conventional automatic transmission fluid and the filter should be changed about every 20,000 miles in RV use. If cooling is marginal and/or the fluid has been overheated, the transmission fluid should be changed every 10,000 miles during the period when high temperatures occur.

The use of extended-life fluid such as Dexron III can permit longer change intervals. A 50,000-mile maintenance interval is recommended by Chevrolet for late-model motorhome chassis in which Dexron III is used as factory fill.

"Chevrolet's Motorhome Chassis Service Guide" states that the

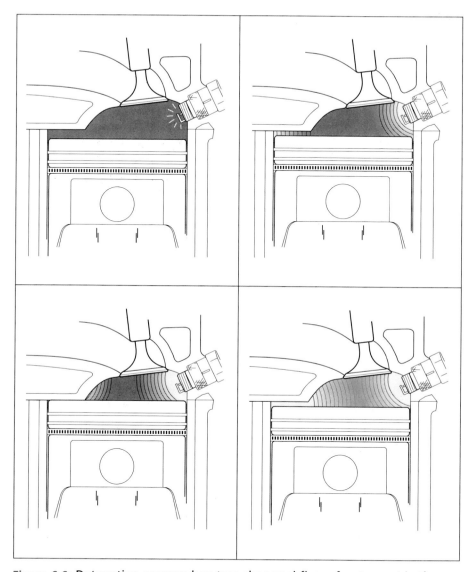

Figure 6.6: Detonation occurs when two abnormal flame fronts meet in the combustion chamber, creating shock waves and the sound of spark knock or "ping."

color and odor of Dexron III are not as reliable for the indication of overheated fluid as was the case with fluids of older design. The fluid may take on a brownish color without having deteriorated. However, if the fluid has an odor similar to burned electrical equipment or contains solid particles, you should have the transmission checked and serviced at once.

MANUAL TRANSMISSION OIL

Standard transmissions (and four-wheel-drive transfer cases) have no gauges or warning lights and often get ignored until it's too late. Check the fluid level every time the engine oil is changed, and change the oil in the gearbox at the intervals recommended in the maintenance section of the owner's manual. Use the correct viscosity, such as 80W-90, for the expected climactic conditions.

Synthetic gear lubricants are now available and generally offer reduced operating temperatures and longer component life. Read the owner's manual for the manufacturer's recommendations on use of synthetics in limited-slip differentials.

DETONATION AND PREIGNITION

Spark knock is the audible portion of either detonation or preignition. It can be caused by different conditions, but the results are similar: extreme stress and heat leading to engine damage. Detonation occurs when a rapid rise in temperature or pressure ignites the air-fuel mixture. This premature combustion pushes the piston down violently while it's still being pushed up by the crankshaft and connecting rod. Preignition has the same result, but the abnormal flame front may be ignited by a glowing piece of metal or carbon *(Figure 6.6)*.

Engine ping typically occurs under heavy loads and high temperatures. Although a slight ping on initial acceleration or at the moment of upshift under heavy load is not cause for alarm, continued and heavy pinging may do damage. As the combustion-chamber temperature increases beyond normal in an engine that has a tendency to ping, higher fuel octane may be needed. If spark knock is allowed to continue, the abnormal combustion that results can in severe cases put holes in tops of pistons. Piston-ring seal may be disturbed, and valve and valve-seat wear is accelerated.

Most late-model cars and light trucks are equipped with "knock" sensors that detect engine ping or spark knock, telling the computer to retard the spark timing. If your engine is not equipped with a knock sensor, it's important to recognize that detonation can substantially shorten the life of your engine.

In addition to excessive temperature and inadequate fuel octane, excessively lean air-fuel ratios can cause ping. Whatever the cause, the problem must be avoided. Cures include improved engine cooling, improved exhaust flow, higher fuel octane, exhaust gas recirculation system repair, and reduction of initial spark advance.

COOLDOWN

When an engine is operated under heavy throttle for an extended period, such as while climbing a mountain grade, temperatures should be allowed to restabilize before shutdown. Turbochargers and exhaust manifolds are particularly at risk to hot shutdown, but it also can compromise gasket sealing and other parts such as intake manifolds. Hot shutdown can cause coolant after boil and fuel percolation (engine flooding) in carbureted engines.

The most severe high temperature shutdown situation occurs in hot weather after climbing a mountain grade that has a turnout at the top. When stopping in such situations, allow the engine to idle for three to five minutes in park, (or, neutral, with manual transmission) before shutdown, preferably with the hood up to improve air circulation.

REFORMULATED GASOLINE

The federal government mandated the use of reformulated gasoline nationwide in mid-1996. The result is fuels that include alcohol or other agents to promote cleaner combustion and reduce emissions. Another result was lower heat content and a change in air/fuel ratios in vehicles without electronic feedback fuel systems, which are designed to maintain pre-programmed air/fuel ratios regardless of changes in fuel.

Thus the only vehicles that are vulnerable to damage are those with carburetors. Leaner fuel mixtures create more heat and increase the tendency of the engine to spark knock. Problems can range from a drop in fuel mileage and deteriorated rubber parts in the fuel system to cracked manifolds, burned exhaust valves, broken piston rings, and damaged pistons.

If the engine runs too lean, it's necessary to have the carbureter recalibrated internally (different metering rods and jets) based on chassis dynomometer testing.

ENGINE-SERVICE INTERVALS

Even while we search for new ways to stretch engine life, engineers say that one of the primary causes of engine wear is poor engine maintenance. Many owners apparently stretch service intervals through inattention or by misreading the owner's manual. Most manufacturers of engines specify two sets of maintenance intervals—one for typical use and another for severe use.

General Motors, for example, recommends oil changes every 3,000 miles or three months for severe service rather than the 7,500 miles or twelve months prescribed for normal driving. The GM diesel schedule calls for oil and filter changes every 2,500 miles or three months for severe service and 5,000 miles or twelve months under normal driving conditions.

Severe service is defined as operating in dusty areas, towing a trailer, extended idling and/or frequent low-speed operation such as in stop-and-go traffic, operating when outside temperatures remains below freezing, and when most trips are less than four miles. Even though it's not specifically mentioned, the weight of motorhomes subjects their chassis to severe service.

Other manufacturers have similar schedules designed to recognize severe versus normal service.

Oil Filters

Filtration of oil is critical to remove abrasive particles that come from engine components, as well as those that may leak through the air-filtration system. The standard pleated paper filters are designed to catch particles down to about 25 microns in size *(Figure 6.7)*. A micron is about 1/25,000 inch.

For greatest engine durability, you should use a name-brand filter and change it according to the vehicle manufacturer's recommendation.

Figure 6.7: Standard, pleated, paper oil filters are designed to remove contaminants down to approximately 25 microns in size.

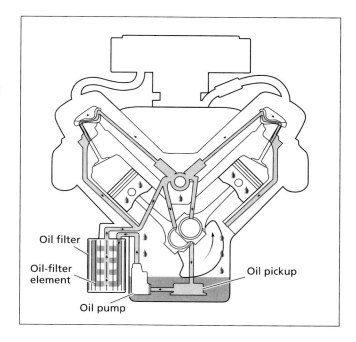

Air Filters

The air-filter element should be inspected every 10,000 miles or less if the vehicle has been used in dusty conditions. Also, look for restrictions in the fresh-air inlet tube. Hoses sometimes collapse, and foreign matter can partially block the inlet.

Pumping Losses

Engine efficiency affects more than fuel economy and performance, it also affects longevity. Parasitic losses occur in several ways, at least one of which may be altered by the owner. Such inefficiencies include pumping losses—excessive suction on the intake side of an engine and excessive back pressure in the exhaust chambers. Others include piston-ring drag and friction in bearings, cams, lifters, valve steps, and seals.

All engines must create a partial vacuum with the intake stroke of the piston in order to draw in air or an air/fuel mixture. But, when a piston must act against excessive partial vacuum (restricted air intake), the partial vacuum adds to the load of the piston. More horsepower from the crankshaft must be used to move the piston on its intake stroke.

TIPS THAT WORK

Dry As a Bone

If you personally change the motor oil in your tow vehicle or motorhome, you are well acquainted with the confident feeling that the job was done right. The one cautionary step overlooked by nearly everyone doing his own oil change is prefilling the new oil filter prior to installation. Not even all the pros do it.

A dry filter means that the engine's oil pump cannot pressurize internal oil galleys until this 1- to 2-quart void is filled. Simply put, by failing to perform this important oil-change step, you can force your vehicle's engine to run for up to 30 oil-starved seconds *before* wear-preventing lubricant can reach vital parts.

Thankfully, it's a simple matter to avoid this unnecessary period of accelerated engine wear. All you have to do is top off the filter with oil before you spin it into place. (A word of caution: Be certain to deduct the amount of oil used for this purpose from the total engine-fill specifications. If you don't, an overfilled crankcase will result.)

As might be imagined, this job is easily accomplished if the filter mounts vertically on the engine. However, it is slightly more time-consuming and tricky if your power plant has its filter canister placed in a near-horizontal plane.

When filling these filters, pour the oil in a little at a time, turning the container on its side and rotating so the dry element material can absorb as much of the lubricant as possible. Continue pouring only until the oil level reaches the bottom of the threaded opening as the filter is held in the horizontal plane. Be careful not to overfill, or you'll experience spillage during filter installation.

Adopting this prefill precaution requires only a small extra effort. The reward for your thoroughness is near-instant lubrication at engine start-up, and a power plant undamaged by owner-induced oil starvation.

Richard Mater
Santa Maria, California

Likewise, excessive exhaust back pressure causes excessive pumping loss as the piston exerts pressure on the gases to force them out the exhaust. Again, horsepower from the crankshaft must be used to overcome back pressure and create exhaust flow. The energy for these pumping losses must be provided by fuel. The pumping losses add to loads on pistons, cylinders, and bearings. Reducing pumping losses allows the engine to devote more energy to propelling the vehicle.

EFFECTS OF STORAGE

Some RVs, particularly motorhomes, are stored for long periods during winter months. Long-term storage can be hard on an engine if preventive maintenance is not performed.

The engine oil and filter should be changed immediately before the vehicle is put into storage. This prevents the acids in the oil from doing their corrosive work on bearings during the storage period. Also, proper amounts of fuel additive should be poured into the gasoline tank to prevent fuel deterioration and formation of varnishes on surfaces in fuel systems, particularly injector nozzles and carburetor components. This is particularly important with oxygenated fuels. Fuel-storage additives are sold in auto-parts stores.

The vehicle should be driven for a few minutes to circulate the oil and the additive-protected fuel. Just prior to parking the vehicle, idle the engine and inject enough light oil into the carburetor or EFI intake to produce smoke from the exhaust. This coats the cylinders to prevent rust. Boating-supply stores sell oil designed for this purpose. Shut the engine down after the smoke appears. During the storage period the engine should not be started because this wipes away the oil coating in the cylinders and also causes formation of water in the crankcase and exhaust system due to condensation.

Be sure to use enough fuel additive to protect the entire contents of the tank. It's best to store the vehicle with the fuel tank full to minimize water formation due to condensation. A complete chassis lubrication and check-out should also be performed. Tires should be inflated to normal pressures for travel. Provisions should be made for battery charging once a month unless the battery is a gel type that does not self-discharge as rapidly as an open-cell battery.

DIESEL ENGINES

Dependability, durability, and economy of the diesel engine is unquestioned. The heavy-duty diesels in commercial truck service routinely go beyond the 400,000-mile mark before requiring a major overhaul. Many engines used in motorhomes—Cummins, Caterpillar, Detroit Diesel—have the same kind of longevity. The lighter-duty turbocharged engines, such as the GM 6.5-liter, the Ford/Navistar 7.3-liter and the Cummins 5.9-liter used in Dodge pickups, should provide 250,000 or more miles before major repair is needed.

This longevity does not occur from simply owning a diesel; a strict regimen of thoughtful preventive maintenance, coupled with sensible operating habits, is essential to realize this potential.

Diesel-Fuel Systems

Preventive maintenance of diesel-fuel systems is basically simple, but very small tolerances are used in injector pumps and components. For example, if the plunger and bushing were separated from a Detroit Diesel injector in a room with 65°F ambient temperature, and the plunger was held in a person's hand for two minutes, it could not be reinserted in the bushing due to thermal expansion. And the sweat from your hand could damage the lapped surface if not cleaned off within a few minutes. This serves to illustrate why the cardinal rule in fuel-system care is to "keep it clean." A microscopic bit of sand can render a $200 injector useless. Yet this same injector could last the service life of the engine with good preventive maintenance.

Some diesel-fuel systems include two filters for protecting the injection pump and the injectors, but most have one, a combination water separator and final filter *(Figure 6.8)*. Other engines have water separator/primary filters in the suction side of the fuel-transfer pump, and a final filter between the fuel-transfer pump and injection pump.

Figure 6.8
On most late-model diesel engines, a single unit serves as both the fuel filter and the water separator.

Sediment filters have the capability of removing particles as small as 80 to 100 microns (.0032 inch to .004 inch), and the final filter can be as fine as 5 microns (.0002 inch). The better sediment filters have a glass or clear plastic bowl that enables you to see how much water or other crud has accumulated. The only problem with the plastic bowls is when the sediment filter is mounted outside the frame rail and near the ground, road debris can abrade the plastic so badly it becomes opaque. If you do have one mounted, place it where it is protected and visible. "Out of sight, out of mind" can apply when a sediment filter is hidden from view.

Some sediment filters also have sensing devices that trigger a light on the dash, warning of high water level. Don't rely on the light to tell you when to drain or clean the filter. It should be checked, either by visual inspection or draining, at least weekly. If you travel in the boondocks and must buy fuel from local suppliers, check it daily, preferably at the day's end, at least an hour after shutdown. You may be surprised how much trash you find in it. You could take on a load of contaminated fuel twelve miles or twenty-two minutes after a scheduled filter change. Carry a couple of spares, know how to install them, and know how to bleed the fuel system. Changing a filter need not be a frustrating experience. Just remember, clean.

Most manufacturers do not recommend filling a new filter with fuel prior to installation, to reduce the chance of fuel contamination. However, when done right, there is little chance of getting dirt in the fuel. Priming a new filter can make a restart much easier. Some engines will reprime their fuel systems easily; some will not.

To prime a filter, *(Figure 6.9)* fill a clear plastic container with fuel, cover it, and let it set for at least an hour to allow any sediment or water to settle to the bottom. Then slowly pour this fuel through a clean, drip coffee filter into another clean, nonmetallic container. After removing the old filter, clean the filter base to reduce the chance of any dirt falling into the new filter, then remove the old filter. Unwrap the new filter, fill it with the priming fuel, wait a few seconds to let the filter media absorb the fuel, then finish filling it. Coat the filter gasket with clean grease or petroleum jelly and install the filter. Do not over-tighten, or you may crush the gasket and cause a leak. Fire it up and check for leaks. You may get a burp or two, then the engine should run smoothly. If it does not start, loosen the vent on top of the filter base and have your helper crank the engine until an uninterrupted stream of fuel comes from the vent, then close it. The engine should now run smoothly.

Bacteria

Warm, humid weather can cause fuel problems. A bacterial growth nicknamed "fuel fungus" or "black slime" grows in the interface between the fuel and any water that may be in the tanks or filters. This is not algae, as algae needs light to grow, but it closely resembles it. This slimy mess that can completely plug a filter causes power loss and can even shut down the engine. Once formed, it is difficult to eradicate and is more prevalent in storage or fuel tanks that sit idle for a week or more.

The best prevention is not getting water into the tanks in the first place, but this is sometimes inevitable. The next-best solution is addition of a fungicide formulated for diesel fuel. Regular fuel additives, or antigel agents, usually do not have a fungicide in them, and the fungicide can be hard to find on the open market. The addition of kerosene, gasoline, or acceptable alcohols does not help. If you plan on going into the boondocks, you may have to buy fuel wherever you can get it, and your chances of getting water and other contaminants in the fuel are good. *Be prepared: Find a supply of the fungicide and carry it with you.*

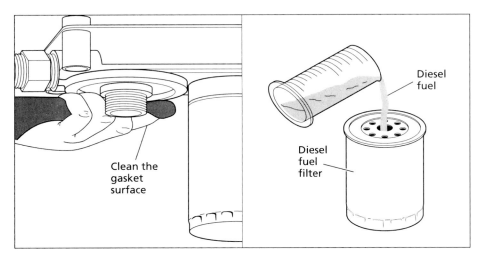

Figure 6.9: Priming the filter can make a diesel engine easier to start following a filter change.

Diesel Lubrication Systems

Diesel engines are much harder on oils than gasoline engines due to the larger amounts of carbon that get into the oil. Carbon is responsible for the dirty, black appearance of the oil and the sulfur/sulfuric acids formed during the combustion process. The carbon is from incompletely burned fuel, and the sulfur comes from the fuel, too. The carbon is not, in itself, very harmful to the engine, other than building up in the various nooks and crannies in the engine and leading to more rapid filter clogging. The sulfur, on the other hand, corrodes iron and bearing metals. The only way to combat these contaminants is through frequent oil and filter changes and by using the best oils available.

Engine condition is also a factor in how fast your oil gets cruddy. An engine with well-seated rings that does not burn a lot of oil doesn't have the ring blow-by that leads to rapid oil contamination. Manufacturers' recommended oil-drain intervals should be followed to the letter, along with use of specified oil grades recommended by the engine manufacturer. Cummins, for example, recommends SAE 15W-40 and a change interval of 6,000 miles or six months for its 5.9- and 8.3-liter engines, suggesting that the multigrade reduces deposits, improves oil flow in cold climates, and improves lubrication during high-temperature operation. Synthetic oils are also approved. Oil analysis as a method of justifying extended oil-drain intervals is specifically not recommended by Cummins.

The recommended oil change for the smaller diesel engines, such as the GM, Ford/Navistar, and Cummins light-truck engines, is 3,000 miles in severe service. (Pulling a trailer or propelling a motorhome is considered severe service.) The big Detroit Diesels have a factory recommendation of 15,000 miles, which seems like an awfully long interval, even for an engine of thirty quarts capacity. But the manufacturer has devoted a great deal of study to oil-change intervals.

Crankcase oil in diesel engines turns black almost immediately, so it's not a good indicator of oil condition. Some folks incorrectly use the appearance of the oil and oil pressure as criteria for oil change. After 3,000 or more miles, if the pressure has not changed, they assume the oil is still good and put another 1,000 miles or so on it. Granted, there may not be excessive carbon in it, but the sulfur count probably is way up there. If the filter has filled with sludge, its bypass valve may have opened and the oil is not going through the filter.

What brand of oil you use is not as important as selecting one with the correct API rating and viscosity. Different brands of oil may vary a bit in their additive packages, and these may vary by locality.

Use name-brand filters. Filter quality varies; Caterpillar, Cummins, Navistar, Ford, and General Motors all assure the effectiveness of their filters. When in doubt about filter quality, use the OEM filter.

The high-quality oils of today need no miracle additives to enhance their performance, and using additives to stretch change intervals is poor economy, not to mention poor preventive maintenance.

Diesel-Engine Coolant

Maintenance of engine coolant is critical for any engine, but especially for diesels. Many diesel-engine manufacturers require special coolant additives to prevent cavitation and pitting of cylinder liners. Follow the engine manufacturer's recommendation on types of coolant, additive, and the change interval. Some manufacturers also require low-silicate antifreeze. Use distilled water in 50–50 percent solution with the coolant, unless the coolant is premixed and needs no water added. Refer to the instruction label.

Diesel Air-Intake Systems

Any engine requires a given volume of air to burn a given amount of fuel. If that air supply is impeded, performance suffers. The air-intake filter must clean this air without starving the engine, and this takes a big, efficient filter—more so on diesels than on gasoline engines, whose air intake is restricted by an air-intake throttle valve. Diesels draw in much more air than gas engines, especially at lower power settings.

Filter types and cleaning methods vary, but regardless of which kind you have, it must be serviced according to the conditions under which the vehicle is used. Many diesel air filters have indicators that signal when service is needed. Most owner's manuals list a cleaning interval, either in miles, hours, or both.

In regular service, this interval may be good enough. But drive through a dust storm, and the recommended interval goes out the window. Frequent inspection is the most foolproof method. If the filter looks dirty, service it; if it doesn't look dirty, but it has been some time since it was last cleaned, check and clean it anyway. If you have the disposable type, carry at least one spare.

Some of the cleanable diesel-engine air filters that come with some aftermarket turbo kits are supplied with one aerosol can of a special oil to re-oil the element. This aerosol can last about three cleanings; then you must locate more. If that proves difficult, make your own oil: Mix your favorite engine oil 50–50 with diesel fuel, and use an empty window-spray bottle to apply it. Whatever type of cleanable filter you have, handle it gently; it is somewhat fragile and banging it on a work bench to dislodge the bugs can distort it or damage the gasket, causing an improper fit, with resultant leakage. Compressed air should not be used on these. A leaking filter is the same as no filter.

ON THE ROAD WITH DIESELS

Anyone who believes in good preventive maintenance knows that a thorough prestart check can prevent a lot of headaches. If the diesel rig is used every day, there should be a daily walkaround inspection routine. The following checklist is not all-inclusive, since all rigs are not the same, but it's a good start.

Startup and Idling Diesels

If everything is okay in the engine house, let's fire it up. Diesels, especially turbocharged diesels, should be run at the slowest speed at which they will idle smoothly until oil pressure stabilizes. Some of the turbos are mounted so they are the last component to receive oil. Since the turbine will spin at startup, high startup rpm may spin the turbo at excessive speed, and premature wear will result. It doesn't do rods or main bearings any good either.

Contrary to legend, extended idling of a diesel engine is detrimental to longevity. Some idling is inevitable, but letting the engine idle for hours is not conducive to long service life. Ideally, you should start the engine, check your instruments to insure everything is A-okay, let the engine idle for a minute to stabilize pressures, then take off at

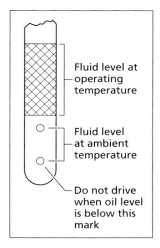

Fluid level at operating temperature

Fluid level at ambient temperature

Do not drive when oil level is below this mark

Figure 6.10: Some dipsticks have different levels for hot and cold operation. Checking the oil level when the engine is hot is preferable.

A DIESEL-ENGINE PRESTART CHECKLIST

❑ If the vehicle has been in storage, perform an engine-oil check when the engine is cold, using the dipstick scale for a cold engine. The rig should be level (very important with Ford/Navistar engines). If the oil level is below the bottom marker, add enough oil slowly to bring it to the bottom marker. In some engines, or in cold weather, it takes a long time for the level to stabilize. Recheck oil level when the engine is fully up to operating temperature and add oil as necessary to bring it to the top marker.

❑ A coolant check should be performed with the engine cold. Check the level in the coolant overflow tank, but also check radiator level; add coolant as needed. If you do not have any coolant mix handy and you must use water, add the same amount of antifreeze at the earliest opportunity; if you have a small leak and must continually add water, you are weakening the coolant protection. If you let small external leaks go until you get around to fixing them, they have a nasty habit of becoming gushers.

❑ Check the automatic transmission. Most manufacturers recommend checking fluid levels while the transmission is at normal operating temperature, and this is good advice. Most dipsticks have a hot and cold level on them, but some folks overlook this (*Figure 6.10*). If you look at the wrong marker at a cold check, you may add fluid when it's not needed; the fluid expands quite a bit as it reaches operating temperature and has been known to overflow out of the dipstick tube onto a hot exhaust pipe or manifold and may catch fire.

❑ Perform a power-steering-fluid check. On dipstick-equipped systems, the stick will have hot and cold levels; again don't overfill the reservoir. Check your owner's manual to determine if your system calls for automatic transmission fluid (ATF) or power steering fluid. ATF and steering fluid have different additives.

❑ Check all drive belts and hoses. Loose belts cause slippage; overtightened belts can cause bearing damage. If you have a loose belt, and you have the correct gauge for measuring tension, great; most folks don't. If you must make a field adjustment, tensioning the belt to $\frac{1}{2}$-inch deflection of the belt between two pulleys will allow you to go on until you can have the belt adjusted properly. Check coolant and any hydraulic hoses for leaks, bulging, soft spots, loose clamps, or leaking fittings. Carrying a spare set of belts and coolant hoses is also considered good preventive maintenance.

❑ Check for leaks. Drips on the ground mean something; any leak is a cause for concern. If you have an engine that is a habitual dribbler and you know the leak source and how often you need to attend to it, fine. But don't be lulled into a false sense of security by the old, familiar dribble.

Note: When starting the engine after prolonged storage, watch the oil-pressure gauge and shut down immediately if pressure doesn't register within fifteen seconds. Check the manufacturer's recommendation.

reduced engine speed until temperatures reach operating level. In very cold temperatures, it may be necessary to let the engine idle; common sense will dictate.

Diesel Cooldown

Allowing a turbocharged diesel engine to idle for three to five minutes before shutdown is essential if the engine has been operated under heavy throttle just prior to stopping. The idling period permits cooldown of superheated components. The flow of lubricating oil through the turbocharger's bearings is halted during a hot shutdown, and the oil may be oxidized by excessive residual heat.

Cold-Weather Care for Diesels

Starting a diesel in cold weather can present some unique problems, particularly at subzero temperatures. The glow-plug-equipped engines, such as Ford/Navistar and General Motors, usually will start at -20°F with little trouble if the engine is in good condition. Other brands like Detroit Diesel, Caterpillar, and Cummins may not have glow plugs (cold-starting devices). In these instances, other starting aids may be required if a 120-volt AC preheater cannot be used. The popular Cummins 5.9-liter engine is equipped with a fuel heater that is controlled thermostatically for cold starts.

Ether-based starting aids, sold in aerosol cans, will get the engine started, but they can damage engines if used in excess; Cummins and several other manufacturers prohibit their use and/or recommend only ether-metering devices. Even when used properly, ether puts a lot of strain on engine parts.

If you must use hand-administered ether, there are right and wrong ways. Removing the air-cleaner cover, firing a long squirt of ether down the engine's throat, then racing back to the cab to hit the starter is not the right way. In this method, you may get a heavy dose of ether into one or two cylinders whose intake valves are open, and little, if any, in the other cylinders. Have someone crank the engine while you fire short bursts of ether into the air intake. This will give each cylinder a more balanced dose. You may have to give the engine a couple more short bursts to keep it running.

There are other ways to get the balky engine started in an emergency. If you have 120-volt AC power available, using a hair dryer can help; set it on the hottest setting and direct the airflow into the air intake.

Diesel Storage

Some folks "lay up" their diesel rig in winter for three to six months with little preventive care. A biocide agent should be added to diesel fuel before storage.

On all models, the oil and filter should be changed, and tire pressure should be checked. The fuel tanks should be topped off to minimize air space with resultant condensation. With the engine and oil warm, run the engine at about half speed, and while still running, squirt a liberal quantity of a light oil, preferably a preservative oil, into the intake. Shut the engine down while it is still smoking to create a thin film of oil on the cylinder walls and exhaust system to prevent rust. Seal off the intake and exhaust pipes before the engine cools. Be sure to remove the seals prior to restarting!

Charge batteries in the vehicle once a month (every six months with gel-type batteries), or remove them for storage in a heated area. Use a maintenance-type float charger to keep the batteries up.

In summary, getting the best longevity, dependability, and fuel economy from an engine requires effort. If you give the engine the care it deserves, it will repay you with trouble-free, dependable performance.

TIPS THAT WORK

The Diesel Trap

Many RVers are using diesel-powered tow vehicles these days. Some also encounter problems with slow starting. While there are several possibilities that can cause such a condition, one which is often overlooked is a drain leak in the fuel/water separator housing.

When the vehicle is parked, fuel can drip out of a defective drain valve, lowering the fuel level inside the separator. When this happens, the engine must be cranked longer to refill this container, which could burn out the starter. Replacement of a factory fuel-water separator assembly can be expensive. However, this isn't necessary. For about $2, a simple 1/4- or 3/8-inch shutoff valve can be installed in the existing drain line using a 1/2-inch hose clamp. This will stop the unwanted fuel leak.

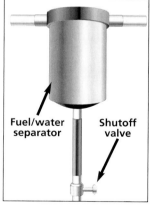

Fuel/water separator   Shutoff valve

Also, you can avoid prolonged starter use when it is necessary to drain contaminated fuel from the separator. Just unscrew the water sensor, and fill the reservoir to the top with clean diesel fuel. The engine should start quickly. Do the same after replacing the fuel filter.

John G. Warlick
Richmond, VA

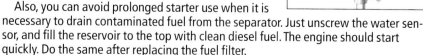

Troubleshooting RV Engines

In this chapter the following items will be covered:

- Be Prepared
- General Troubleshooting for All Engines
- Additional Troubleshooting for Diesel Engines Only

*V*ehicle breakdowns on the road are at least vexing and can be expensive, frightening, and even hazardous. The best prevention is a comprehensive scheduled maintenance program and thorough pre-trip inspection, which can save you time and money in the long run. However, with even the best maintenance, the possibility still exists that your RV may balk unexpectedly.

To loosely paraphrase an old saying: An ounce of diagnosis is worth a pound of money. This chapter, with its accompanying troubleshooting procedures, covers the most common vehicle failures, whether the rig is powered by diesel or gasoline. It will give you some helpful hints designed to get you going again. Certainly there are many things that could go wrong on the road, but failures in the systems covered here—fuel, ignition, and cooling—account for most on-the-road troubles.

This chapter has covered basic on-the-road trouble situations so you can diagnose malfunctions, which should be informative whether you attempt to repair the problems or seek help from a professional mechanic. Many detailed automotive troubleshooting books are available at dealerships, in libraries, and bookstores. Shop manuals from the manufacturer for the specific vehicle are great to have; even if they are too advanced for you, often they can be of use to a mechanic if a breakdown occurs where there is no franchised dealer. Being informed is important. While most mechanics are honest, the motorist who is totally ignorant of the causes of a mechanical breakdown is a more likely target and may pay for unneccessary repairs.

BE PREPARED

To make the troubleshooting procedures work for you, a basic set of tools should be on board. It doesn't have to be a full-blown set weighing hundreds of pounds and costing thousands of dollars; just the basics will do. Be sure to get the right types of tools for your vehicle. Older American-built vehicles use standard (fractional inch-based) tools; all imported and late-model American-built vehicles use metric sizes and many American-built vehicles use a combination of metric and standard fasteners. A good set for travel should consist of:

- Combination wrenches, (both open and box end) standard from ⅜ to 1 inch or metric 8 mm to 24 mm
- Several common sizes each of flat-blade and Phillips screwdrivers

- A ⅜-inch-drive ratchet set with sockets from ⅜ inch to ¾ inch or 6 mm to 19 mm
- A ½-inch-drive socket set from ½ inch to 1 inch
- A set of Torx bits
- Needlenose and regular pliers, plus slip-joint "water-pump" pliers
- Locking pliers such as Vise Grips®
- A one-pound hammer
- A pocket knife
- Spark-plug socket (check your engine's size, either ⅝ inch or ¹³⁄16 inch)
- A good set of high-quality, long, heavy-duty jumper cables
- An electrical test light, or better yet, a digital multimeter (volt-ohm meter)
- Lengths of spare electrical wire in several gauge sizes, a wire crimper, butt connectors, and wire splicers
- A flashlight with spare batteries

Every RVer should carry along a few spare parts as well, including:

- Spare engine drive belts. Whether your rig is a $250,000 diesel coach or a $20,000 gasoline-powered pickup truck, it can't function without a simple and inexpensive drivebelt.
- Spare fuel filter(s). One tank of dirty or water-contaminated fuel can render the rig helpless.
- Extra upper and lower radiator hoses, hose clamps and at least four feet of spare heater hose
- A can of radiator stop-leak
- A new set of distributor points and condenser (in the unlikely event you are still driving a vehicle with a conventional ignition system). A spare distributor cap and rotor could also save the day.
- A roll of duct tape and a few clean rags
- Spare fuses that not only fit the 12-volt DC RV accessories, but will fit any engine or chassis circuitry. Spare fusible links are also invaluable.
- It's also a good idea to carry a couple extra quarts of motor oil and automatic transmission fluid, plus a fresh, unopened can of brake fluid.

TIPS THAT WORK

Getting Belted

Thaaawunk! You hear a strange, muffled sound from somewhere near the engine. It only lasts a second or two. Only slightly startled, you continue on your way. Then, you notice the glare of the little red alternator light on the dash. Then, the engine overheat bulb snaps to life. Bad news: One or more of the engine's drive belts is going AWOL.

It's possible to travel some distance during daylight hours without a functioning alternator. Just turn off all electrical equipment and drive to the next repair facility. Not so without the water pump.

However, there is a chance you can extricate yourself from this dilemma with a single pair of women's nylon hose (not panty hose). Start by gaining access to the front of the RV's engine. Clear any belt debris from the pulley track. This done, wrap one leg of the hosiery around the crankshaft pulley (bottom-most pulley), and stretch it tightly around the corresponding water-pump pulley (the one attached to the fan). Tie off your handiwork with a tight square knot made as small as possible.

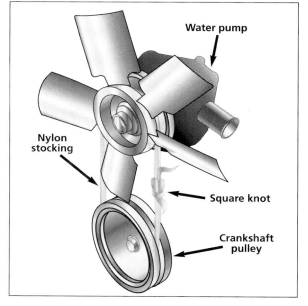

Don't try to get fancy and drive accessories other than the water pump with this makeshift setup. The nylons will fail quickly, if you do.

Also, if the only product your donor has to sacrifice is panty hose, make sure you first cut off the panty portion before attempting this fix. You won't get far if you try wrapping a complete, uncut pair around the engine pulleys. If you have a choice, support hose are even better than regular.

While the finished repair won't look pretty, by driving slowly you can probably keep the water pump churning long enough to reach help (watch the temperature gauge). The lesson here is to carry spare belts on your next trip.

Troubleshooting Gasoline Engines

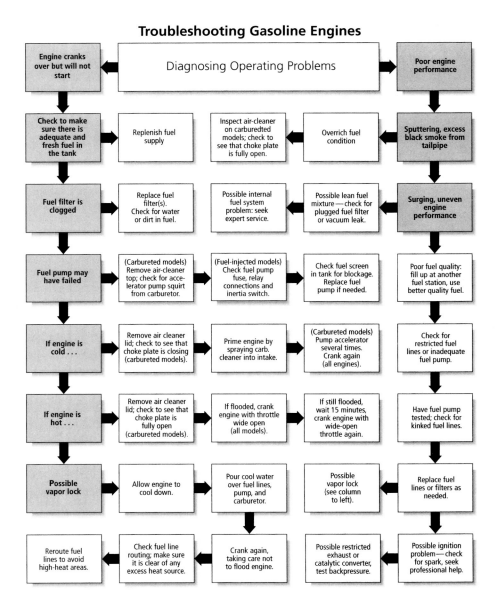

Figure 7.1: Locating the source of a problem with a gasoline engine requires a step-by-step troubleshooting process. *(See Figure 7.6 on page 172 for troubleshooting diesel engines.)*

Although this is a basic "bare-bones" spare-parts assortment that will probably get you going in event of emergency, these supplies and tools can be absolutely invaluable. Even if you are not the mechanical type, you may be able to get another RVer or a shop to install a part that you carried, which was not available in the area of the breakdown.

GENERAL TROUBLESHOOTING FOR ALL ENGINES

If Engine Fails to Start

For your engine to run, three systems must operate in harmony, assuming it hasn't experienced a major internal failure like a thrown rod. 1. The starting system must be able to crank the engine; 2. The fuel system must supply the proper amount of fuel to the engine; 3. The ignition system (gasoline engines only) must supply sufficient voltage to the spark plugs to initiate combustion. The troubleshooting procedures in Figure 7.1 will take you through each of these areas and give you points to check in order to single out the culprit.

Since many more problems occur than can be listed here, the procedures cover only the most common problems—those that lend themselves to roadside repair.

Checking the Battery

If an engine won't start, we must systematically eliminate possible causes. If the engine simply fails to crank or cranks too slowly, check the battery terminals for corrosion and/or looseness. If the terminal connections are heavily corroded, they should be removed and scraped clean with a knife. Or, purchase a battery brush/terminal cleaner and keep it in the toolbox. Sometimes a starter will begin working or crank faster after it cools.

Caution: *When working around the battery, acid can cause burns to skin and eyes and ruin clothes. Take care to avoid exposure, and if it occurs, immediately wash the area with water and, if it has affected eyes, seek medical attention.*

To insure that the failure to start is not caused by dirty battery components, thoroughly clean the battery and terminals.

Next, try to start the engine. If there is no activity from the starter, turn on the headlights and check them for brightness. If they are dim, the battery charge is low and will require a jump-start, battery recharge, or battery replacement. Some RVs, mainly large

AN IGNITION-SYSTEM CHECKLIST FOR GASOLINE ENGINES

When checking the ignition system of a gasoline engine, follow these steps:

1. Remove a spark-plug cable from a plug, or remove the center cable from the distributor cap. Some ignitions may not have a center cable to the distributor cap because the coil assembly is actually built into the distributor.

2. Turn on the ignition switch, and have someone crank the engine while you hold a spark-plug cable (using insulated pliers) against a good ground *(Figure 7.2)*, which is any metal engine part. There should be an obvious spark every other engine revolution. If there is a strong spark, the source of the problem probably is in the fuel system. If no spark is present, remove the distributor cap and make sure there is no moisture inside. If you are near 120-volt-AC power, or if you have an AC generator, you can dry the distributor with an electric hair dryer. If that's not possible, dry the cap and as many ignition components that you can with paper towels or a clean, absorbent rag.

3. Replace the dry cap and try the spark test again. If no spark is present, replace the spark-plug cable and determine whether your system is electronic or the old style with breaker points.

motorhomes, have battery-boost circuits that allow you to bring the vehicle's auxiliary battery(ies) into parallel with the starting battery by pushing a switch. This is invaluable, especially if you have forgotten to turn off chassis accessories such as the headlights. If you don't have a battery-booster switch circuit, use a set of top-quality jumper cables to connect the auxiliary battery to the engine battery.

If, after cleaning the terminals and attempting a jump-start, the engine still fails to crank, the problem is probably in the starter itself or its circuitry. Troubleshooting beyond this point will probably require the aid of a professional mechanic with specialized test equipment.

Figure 7.2:
To check for
spark, insert a
spare spark
plug in any
cable, hold it
against a
metal part
while engine
is cranked.

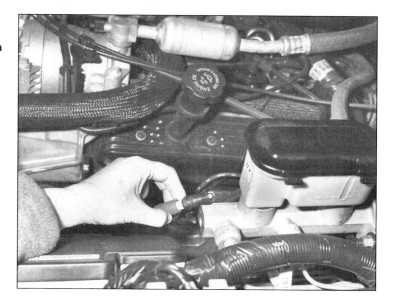

Check the Ignition and Fuel System

If terminal cleaning and jump-starting bring the starter to life, but the engine still fails to start, new tactics are needed. When the engine is gasoline-powered, the trouble can be narrowed to the ignition system or fuel system. If the engine is diesel, the fuel and preheating systems are the only places you'll need to look since diesels don't have ignition systems.

First things first. Check the fuel gauge! If you have any reason to doubt the fuel gauge, tap on the tank with your knuckles and listen for an empty, hollow sound. Remove the filler cap and listen for a whoosh that indicates a possible venting problem. This may seem obvious, but many professional mechanics have wasted time troubleshooting a vehicle that fails to start or run without first checking the basics.

Electronic ignition systems are normally reliable and maintenance free. When they fail, usually only the replacement of faulty components will get you rolling. However, there are a few things a novice mechanic can do. Look for any burned or damaged wires around the ignition components. Remove the distributor cap and check for cracks inside, check the rotor, and closely examine the wires connected to the ignition pickup and module; often they break internally due to constant flexing. Also look over the coil for cracks or damage.

Figure 7.3
Visual checks
for presence
of fuel are
possible on
carbureted or
throttle-body
fuel injection-
equipped
engines.

Checking for Fuel Delivery

If the fuel tank appears to contain enough fuel, check to see if the fuel is getting to the engine. In gasoline-carbureted engines checking for fuel delivery is easy, but in diesel or fuel-injected gasoline engines it can be more difficult.

1. First, remove the air-cleaner cover to expose the air horn of the carburetor or throttle body of a fuel-injection system (this procedure is not applicable to port-type fuel-injection systems).

2. If the engine is carbureted, use a flashlight to look into the carburetor throat *(Figure 7.3)*. Hold the choke plate open, and have an assistant slowly depress the throttle. Check for fuel squirting into the primary carburetor bores—the bore(s) that have choke plates). Squirting fuel is the result of the action of the accelerator pump. If no fuel squirts when the throttle is pumped, the fuel bowl of the carburetor is probably empty, or the accelerator pump may be defective.

3. In the case of a carbureted or throttle-body fuel-injected engine, have the assistant turn the ignition key on and off a couple of times while you look into the throttle body. If no fuel is present, crank the engine for two or three seconds, and repeat the check for fuel at the carburetor or throttle body. If still no fuel is present, the fuel pump may be inoperative, the fuel filter may be clogged, or vapor lock may be the culprit, especially if ambient temperature is high.

4. If your RV has an electric fuel pump inside the fuel tank, check the owner's manual for the fuse location and inspect the fuse. Also check the owner's manual for the location and reset procedure for a fuel pump cutoff switch (these are common on Fords with fuel injection). Have an assistant turn the ignition key on (but not to the start position) for a few seconds and then off while you listen for the sound of the pump running. If the pump runs and the fuse is okay, but fuel still is not present at the engine, a fuel pump relay may be faulty. Have a professional mechanic check the fuel system.

5. If the fuel filter is suspected, it is usually easily changed. Many carburetors have inlet filters that can be removed, while other vehicles may have in-line filters between the pump and carburetor or between the tank and pump. Check carefully along the length of the chassis where the fuel lines are routed. Wear eye protection, and be especially careful on fuel-injected vehicles because they often retain pressure even after they're shut off. In any case, hot engine parts and dripping fuel can spell disaster. Make sure that you take precautions to prevent fire when working with the fuel system. Let the engine cool, keep a fire extinguisher handy, and by all means, no smoking!

6. On fuel-injected engines, if you are not sure if it's getting fuel, spray a little aerosol carburetor cleaner into the intake. Crank the engine. If it now starts and runs briefly, the problem is somewhere in the fuel-supply system.

Checking for a Faulty Fuel Pump on a Carbureted Engine

1. Disable the ignition system so the engine will not start. The best way to do this is to remove the 12-volt lead to the coil or the distributor.

2. Remove the fuel line from the carburetor. Hold a container at the end of the open line at the carburetor and have someone briefly crank the engine. Fuel should pulsate from the line. If it does not, the pump is bad, the filter or fuel-tank pickup is clogged, or the engine is still vapor locked. Again, be aware of fire danger.

3. Look at the fuel in the container to see if it has water or dirt in it. Also sniff it to determine if the vehicle may have been misfueled with diesel fuel.

Checking Fuel Delivery to Gasoline Fuel-Injected Engines

Fuel delivery to electronic fuel-injection (EFI) systems is more difficult to diagnose. Fuel pressure typically ranges from 9 psi to 45 psi,
depending on the model, versus 5 psi to 7 psi for carbureted engines.
This creates the possibility that significant volumes of fuel can be
sprayed in the engine compartment if you make an error during pressure testing. If your EFI-equipped engine has a fuel-delivery problem,
see Chapter 4 for a method of checking pressure. Beyond that, contact
your dealer or a professional mechanic who is proficient in the repair
of EFI systems.

Fuel-Tank-Cap Problems

Fuel-tank-cap problems can plague RV engines. The wrong cap or a
clogged or damaged one can cause the engine to starve for fuel, especially under high-demand situations like climbing steep grades. If the
cap is not properly vented, air cannot enter the tank, and a partial
vacuum forms, making it impossible for the fuel pump to do its job. If
frequent fuel-starvation problems are noted, make sure that the gas
cap is the right one. An easy way to test the cap is by loosening it and
driving the vehicle under the same conditions that usually cause trouble. If the problem is solved, get a new, correct cap.

Vapor Lock (Gasoline Only)

Hot weather can cause vapor lock by boiling the gasoline before it
can reach the fuel pump, or after it has passed the pump on the way
to the engine. Pouring cool water over the fuel lines and pump will
condense the fuel back into its liquid state. Vapor lock is less likely
with fuel-injected systems because fuel in the entire system is under
pressure, raising the vaporization point. However, it can occur on
some fuel-injection systems, particularly upstream of the fuel pump.
Also, some electric fuel pumps slow or quit when they get hot.

A vapor-lock problem is indicated if your engine quits when the
weather is very warm but runs well when it cools down. However, ignition problems can mimic vapor lock. Check for spark immediately
after the engine quits; if there's no spark or a weak spark, check the
coil and electronic components in the ignition system.

If vapor lock is a persistent problem, heat buildup in the engine
compartment is likely, due to poor ventilation, or the fuel lines may be

exposed to heat radiation from the engine (especially exhaust components), causing the fuel to vaporize in the line. Make sure fuel lines are insulated and routed well away from any excessive heat source. Use procedures described on page 162 to check for fuel delivery.

Flooding in Gasoline Engines

So much for lack of fuel, what about flooding of gasoline engines? The first sign that an engine is operating under a high fuel-to-air ratio (rich condition) is the presence of black smoke from the exhaust. Make sure that you don't confuse it with blue smoke, which is a sign the engine is burning oil. Black smoke is accompanied by sluggish performance and very poor fuel economy.

If your RV is equipped with a carburetor, a choke plate that is stuck closed or is not adjusted correctly is the most common cause of an over-rich condition. Remove the air-cleaner lid and inspect the choke plate with the engine at normal operating temperature. The plate should be in a vertical (open) position to allow free flow of air through the carburetor. If the plate is closed on a warm engine, it partially blocks the airflow, causing the rich condition. The plate should be nearly closed when the engine is cold to enrich the fuel mixture.

If the plate refuses to open when the engine is warmed, it's possible to keep it open by temporarily wiring the choke linkage in the open position. This is a temporary fix that allows you to drive the vehicle, albeit with difficult cold starts. Make sure that your temporary choke wiring cannot cause the throttle linkage to jam, which could cause engine overspeed and a dangerous situation. Other causes of an over-rich condition cannot be easily corrected as they involve other internal circuits of the carburetor.

Other Causes of Flooding

Other fuel problems may be caused by incorrect float adjustment. This allows excess fuel to spill into the engine, causing an over-rich mixture. If your carburetor is equipped with plastic floats, they can become saturated with fuel and raise fuel levels, allowing too much fuel into the engine. In addition to the float, a stuck or blown power valve can cause difficulties. Check with a mechanic if problems with these items are suspected.

Flooding Diagnosis

If you suspect a gasoline engine is flooded but are not sure, remove a spark plug and inspect the firing tip. If it's wet and smells of gasoline, the engine is probably flooded.

Starting a Flooded Gasoline Engine

An engine that is flooded may be difficult to start. When a flooded engine starts, it will emit black smoke from the tailpipe. Make sure that you do not pump the accelerator pedal. This only floods the engine more. On a gas engine, hold the throttle to the floor (wide open) to allow the maximum amount of air to enter the engine. This will tend to dilute the rich fuel mixture. Crank the engine with the throttle in this position for no more than twenty seconds at a time. Continual cranking may overheat and damage the starter motor and will deplete the battery in a short time. If there are no signs of life, wait fifteen minutes and attempt to start again with the throttle held wide open. If results are negative, it may indicate ignition trouble.

You may have to remove all the spark plugs and crank the engine for about twenty seconds to clear fuel out of the combustion chambers.

EFI Troubleshooting

Over-rich mixtures may also occur in EFI systems, but the causes are different. The electronic fuel-control system monitors oxygen content of the exhaust, engine temperature, incoming airflow, and throttle position, just to name a few. A problem with one of these sensing systems can feed the computer incorrect information. A defective temperature sensor may send the computer a signal that the engine is cold, even though it may not be. The computer's reaction is to tell the fuel-injection system to send more fuel, resulting in an unnecessary amount of fuel in the cylinders.

If your EFI engine isn't operating properly, look for any loose, cracked, or missing hoses or damaged wiring. There is little else that can be easily done to analyze the situation since testing of these specific components requires sophisticated equipment and professional knowledge of the particular EFI system. Difficulties in EFI systems are best handled by knowledgeable mechanics.

Overheating in Diesel and Gasoline Engines

There are many causes of engine overheating, some of which can be quite elusive. The following troubleshooting procedures cover the most common overheating causes, many of which can be handled at roadside. Diesel engines seem to have less tendency to overheat compared to gasoline engines, partially because most diesels are outfitted with large, heavy-duty radiators, and less combustion heat is rejected into the coolant.

First, let's define overheating. When is an engine too hot? Technically, an engine is not overheated until it continually boils out through the overflow. But high temperature will cause an engine to operate poorly at temperatures well below the point at which boil out occurs.

Accurate temperature gauges are needed for proper diagnosis of engine temperature. The gauges installed at the factory often are not precisely calibrated. If your RV has an "idiot light" rather than a gauge, or a gauge that is not calibrated in degrees Fahrenheit, install a top-quality gauge calibrated so you can read temperature accurately. By the time a hot-engine warning light is activated, overheating is in advanced stages, which may result in loss of a considerable volume of coolant or engine damage.

When overheating occurs, pull off the road immediately, activate the warning flashers, shift the transmission to "park" or "neutral," set the parking brake, set the heater control on maximum, open the hood, and run the engine at a fast idle (1,500 rpm). If a hose has burst and coolant is pouring out, shut the engine off immediately. Otherwise, if in two or three minutes the temperature has not dropped, it's best to shut the engine off anyway and let it cool.

Once the engine is shut down, coolant loss may be experienced due to after boil (heat soak). When the engine is stopped, the coolant pump and airflow movement provided by engine operation cease, resulting in residual engine heat "soaking" into the stationary coolant, causing it to boil. If coolant is lost every time you shut off the engine, it may mean a defective radiator cap, a weak coolant solution, or an engine that typically runs hot, requiring repairs.

The troubleshooting procedure for overheating cites points in the engine compartment as possible culprits. Make sure the engine accessory-drive belt(s) are tight and in good condition. A loose belt can cause loss of coolant circulation and reduced radiator-fan speed. Belts should be tightened so that moderate pressure with your thumb causes about a ½-inch deflection in the middle of the belt. Make sure all hoses and clamps are checked regularly. Carry spare hoses and belts in your tool set.

A daily walkaround inspection of your RV should include the cooling system. Pop the hood and look at all hose connections and the hoses themselves for signs of leakage. Check the radiator for road debris. It's easy to pick up such things as insects and plastic bags that can block most of the radiator's airflow. Continual neglect can lead to clogging with dirt, bugs, and other debris.

Thermostatic fan clutches must function properly in hot weather *(see Chapter 6)*. It's usually obvious when the clutch engages, as fan noise increases dramatically. Sometimes it sounds like the transmission downshifted. If your RV is overheating and you have a fan clutch, it should engage as the temperature rises and disengage as the temperature drops. If you don't hear the cycling action of the fan, the clutch may be defective.

If you're trapped in stop-and-go traffic and the engine starts to overheat, idle speed may be set too low. Slow idle speeds mean poor coolant circulation and slow airflow past the radiator. Turn off accessories, such as the air conditioner, since it adds heat load to the cooling system. Shift to the neutral position when stopped and run the engine at a fast idle speed (1,500 rpm). If you can stand the heat, set the heater on maximum.

Incorrect engine ignition timing can also contribute to overheating. If ignition timing is excessively retarded, (which may have been done to reduce the engine tendency to spark knock), overheating at low speeds may result. The cure may be to use middle grade or premium fuel so the timing can be returned to the normal setting.

In a few instances, overheating may occur at highway speeds. This is sometimes caused by the collapse of the lower radiator hose. At high pump speeds, there is a strong suction on the inlet to the water pump. Make sure your hose is equipped with a wire coil designed to prevent collapse.

Figure 7.4: A tester is used to check the radiator cap as well as the entire cooling system for pressure retention capability.

Radiator-Cap Problems

It's not commonly known, but a defective radiator cap can cause boil over. The boiling point of the coolant is raised 2.5°F for every pound of pressure added to the system. Most cooling systems use 15-psi caps. Under this pressure, a 50–50 mix of water and ethylene glycol coolant has a boiling point of 265°F. If the cap seal is defective, or if spring pressure is insufficient, the pressure is reduced, allowing the coolant to boil at a lower temperature. Have the cap tested *(Figure 7.4)*.

Water-Pump Failure

Water-pump failure can cause coolant to leak, reducing coolant flow through the engine and radiator. The first sign that the water pump is failing may be slight leakage or bearing noise. The noise is a grumbling sound that may be heard at all speeds and may be particularly noisy at idle. Loss of the water-pump bearings leads to the loss of the water-pump seal, or vice-versa, leading to coolant leakage around the water-pump shaft.

The water pump can also cause overheating. A broken or corroded pump impeller (or one that slips on the shaft) may fail to circulate enough coolant to transfer heat from the engine to the radiator. The reduced ability of the water pump can be checked in the field only by removing the pump and visually inspecting the impeller. With this much work involved, it may be wise to install a new or rebuilt pump.

Other Causes of Overheating

Other not-so-obvious overheating causes can be more serious and may be difficult to detect. Blown head gaskets, cracked cylinder heads, cracked blocks, and coolant leaking into the intake system dictate professional attention. A simple check with a combustion leak detector can spot the presence of exhaust gases in the coolant, which indicates a blown gasket or crack that allows the gases to infiltrate the system. The test will not tell exactly where the leak is occurring, but most often it's a blown head gasket or a crack in the cylinder head, either of which is an expensive item to repair. Leak-detector chemicals, introduced in the radiator, change color to indicate presence of combustion gases. The cooling system must be drained free of antifreeze for the leak detectors to function properly.

The key to preventing overheating is maintenance. Neglect of the cooling system allows rust and scale to form on heat-transferring parts that rid the engine of heat buildup. Use a 50–50 mixture of ethylene glycol and distilled water, unless your vehicle is a late model that requires extended-life coolant and dictates an extended change interval (General Motors vehicles, for example, which require Dex-Cool and stipulate a coolant change every five years or 150,000 miles). Normal coolant should be changed every two years. At coolant-change time it's also a good idea to backflush the cooling system to remove any accumulated sediment. The system-flushing procedure applies to gasoline as well as diesel engines. Diesel owners should check the coolant filter system if the engine is fitted with one. The filter collects debris that may form between changes and backflushing of the system, and it should. Also check your owner's manual for antifreeze specifications, such as silicate content.

ADDITIONAL TROUBLESHOOTING FOR DIESEL ENGINES ONLY

Checking for Lack of Fuel

If the RV's engine is diesel fueled, lack of fuel is almost always caused by a dirty filter. Diesel systems have one and sometimes two filters. Primary and secondary filters are usually connected in series. Some systems use a special water trap just ahead of the primary filter to collect large amounts of water that could find its way into a service station's supply tanks *(Figure 7.5)*.

Lack of fuel is first evident in lack of performance. Diesel-engine power output is directly proportional to the amount of fuel that is injected into the cylinder. Instead of controlling the airflow and fuel flow to the cylinders as a gasoline engine does, diesels control just the amount of fuel that is injected when the piston reaches the top of the compression stroke.

A positive displacement pump that draws its supply from the filter housing supplies fuel to the fuel injectors. If fuel filters become clogged,

Figure 7.5
Trouble with diesels usually can be traced to dirty or water-borne fuel. The water separator is visible at the bottom of this Racor unit.

Troubleshooting Diesel Engines

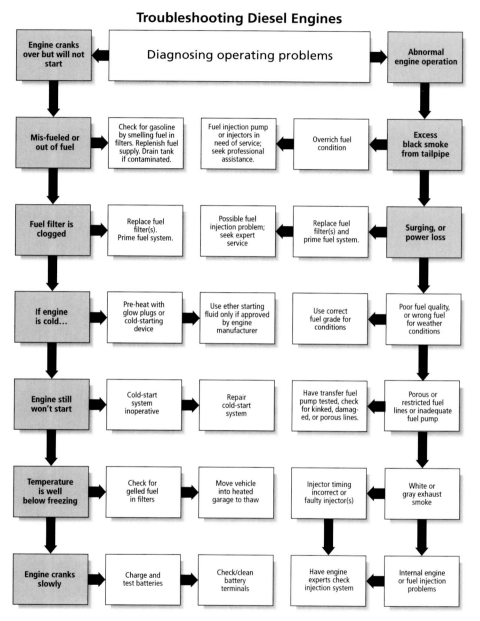

Figure 7.6: Diesel-engine troubleshooting focuses primarily on fuel problems.

they will pass only a fraction of what is necessary to keep the engine operating at peak performance. The engine may idle and run at low speed properly, but at full throttle, performance may drop off. The solution is usually to change both the primary and secondary fuel filters.

If the Diesel Engine Fails to Run

Diesel engines do not require ignition systems. But most diesels do require a preheater, ether injection, or glow plugs to assist in cold starting. If the engine has fuel but still fails to start or run, the next logical place to look is the electrical system.

Checking the Diesel's Glow Plugs

A diesel uses the heat of the compressed air in the combustion chamber to ignite the fuel. The high compression ratios associated with diesel operation heat the air in the chamber enough to ignite the fuel sprayed into the chambers by the injectors.

When the engine is cold, some engines use glow plugs to add enough heat to the combustion chamber to make for easier ignition of the fuel. With age, glow plugs may deteriorate or burn out.

Owners can use a test light to determine if power is getting to the glow plugs during cranking. If no power is getting to the plugs, check for a burned-out glow-plug fuse. Glow plugs may be tested in the field with an ohmmeter; disconnect the glow plug from the circuit and measure the resistance between the terminal on the glow plug and ground. If the resistance is roughly 1 ohm the glow plug is probably okay. If there is an open circuit (infinite resistance), the glow plug is burned out.

Glow-plug circuits can be checked with special testing equipment to determine the condition of the controller and plugs. A diesel-service shop should be able to do this.

Flooding in Diesel Engines

Although flooding usually is associated with carbureted gasoline engines, diesel engines can become flooded too. This usually happens when the driver holds the accelerator pedal down too far while starting a cold engine. It also may occur if the driver doesn't allow the glow plugs or other starting device to warm up before attempting to start the engine.

Typically, a flooded diesel will produce white smoke during crank-ing. Because diesel engines have such high compression, the combus-tion chambers are very small. Therefore, flooding may cause a hydraulic lock in the engine, which may damage the engine. Avoid flooding by following the recommended starting procedure in the owner's manual.

To start a flooded diesel, operate the preheater or glow plugs and crank the engine without stepping on the accelerator pedal. If a diesel is badly flooded, you may have to remove the injectors or glow plugs and crank the engine to clear it.

Checking Fuel Delivery

At least ninety-five percent of all diesel engines that quit on the road are disabled by fuel-supply problems. These breakdowns are usually due to blocked fuel filters, and this is the first item you should check. Often, the engine will gradually lose power, which is noticed first while climbing grades. Unlike a gasoline engine, a diesel with a fuel-filter blockage will run smoothly, but may only run at idle or slightly above. When the blockage gets worse, the engine won't run at all.

Checking and Draining Water Traps in the Fuel System

If water is found, remove the filter(s) and pour their contents into a container. Install fresh fuel filter(s) and follow the instructions in the owner's manual to prime them. Some systems must be primed by a hand pump, and others are primed by cranking the engine. If you fill the filters with diesel fuel prior to installation it will make priming and starting easier.

Look for sediment and give the fuel a "sniff" test. Sometimes diesels are misfueled with gasoline; if this is the case the entire fuel system must be drained.

If no water is found, the filter(s) are full, and the engine still won't start, check for fuel delivery at the injector lines. Wear eye protection and gloves. Have an assistant step on the accelerator pedal about $\frac{1}{4}$ inch, and operate the starter while you use a wrench to slightly loosen the fuel-line fitting at an injector. If fuel is getting this far, you will observe a squirt of fuel every other revolution of the crankshaft. If fuel is squirting from the injector line, it indicates fuel is getting through and the problem probably lies elsewhere. If fuel isn't getting through, carefully check the entire fuel system from tank to injection pump.

If you have followed the previous procedures on checking the fuel filters and for fuel delivery at the injectors and for flooding, yet the engine still won't start or run properly, there are a few more items to check. If the engine seems to crank over slower than normal, the battery may be weak, the starter may be faulty, or the cables or connections are bad.

If these systems are working and the engine cranks over fast enough, there may be an internal problem such as low compression or jumped timing. See Figure 7.6 for diesel troubleshooting procedures.

In cold weather the glow plugs, ether injector, or fuel preheater (if applicable) may not be working or the fuel or oil are too viscous. Diesel engines do not usually suffer from over-rich conditions. If excessive black smoke is evident, the air filter may be plugged or the pump and/or injectors may need repair or adjustment. Professional help should be sought.

RV Electronic Systems

In this chapter the following items will be covered:

- General Electronic Systems Information
- Computer-Controlled Carburetors
- Fuel Injection
- Onboard Computers
- Fuel-Injection Components
- Trouble Codes
- Chrysler/Dodge Trouble Codes

*E*ngines on late-model vehicles can be intimidating. They're nearly hidden by a maze of vacuum hoses, wires, cables, and covered with a variety of unusual-looking components. An onboard computer monitors and controls vital engine and vehicle functions such as fuel delivery, ignition timing, and a multitude of other tasks including climate control, cruise control, and traction control. Initially, it would appear that diagnosis and repair must be left to experts who are trained and specially equipped to deal with such high-tech equipment. These procedures require expensive scan tools, scopes, and exhaust-gas analyzers.

Not quite. The home mechanic can still do a considerable amount of troubleshooting and repair, given specific information and a few simple tools. Even if you don't intend ever to touch your computer-controlled carburetor or electronic fuel-injection (EFI) system, knowledge of its principles and how the components work can be valuable in diagnosing on-the-road problems and finding help, not to mention improving your ability to assess the validity of a repair bill.

GENERAL ELECTRONIC SYSTEMS INFORMATION

Vehicle Emission Control Information Labels

The Vehicle Emission Control Information (VECI) label is required by federal law to be affixed to every emission-controlled vehicle sold in the United States and Canada. This sticker can usually be found on the radiator support, underside of the hood, fan shroud, or rocker-arm cover.

VECI labels provide important information on the specific vehicle you are working on, such as vacuum-hose routing diagrams and tune-up and emission specifications. If any discrepancy exists between the specifications shown in a service manual and the VECI label, trust the label.

Test Equipment

To thoroughly test a computer-equipped vehicle requires thousands of dollars in special equipment, including an oscilloscope, exhaust-gas analyzer, scan tools, and breakout boxes. However, with standard hand tools and a few relatively inexpensive items, such as a 10-megohm impedance digital volt-ohm meter, vacuum gauge, fuel-pressure gauge, and a little persistence, many maladies can be detected.

PRECAUTIONS IN RELIEVING FUEL PRESSURE

The fuel system is pressurized at all times. Be sure to read the following checklist before opening the fuel system:

❑ Remove the fuel-filler caps. With the engine idling, remove the fuel-pump fuse (on Fords, disconnect the wires at the fuel pump), and allow the engine to stall. Wrap a rag around the fittings to soak up any remaining fuel when you open them and always wear eye protection!

❑ When working on fuel systems, always have a fire extinguisher rated for gasoline and electrical fires at hand. Read the instructions!

❑ Never smoke or allow open flames or unprotected light bulbs anywhere near the workplace.

❑ Never work in a closed garage or one with a gas-operated water heater or clothes dryer; the pilot light could ignite fuel vapors.

❑ Keep children and pets away from the work area.

❑ Remember to always wear eye protection when testing or disconnecting fuel-system components.

❑ Do not allow anyone near the driver's controls except a trusted assistant and only when needed during testing.

❑ Remove the keys from the ignition when they are not required for testing.

❑ Always relieve fuel pressure before disconnecting fuel lines and/or fittings.

❑ Never connect or disconnect jumper cables to the battery with the ignition key on.

❑ Before checking compression, disable the fuel-pump circuit by removing the fuse or relay.

❑ Never apply full battery voltage directly to any electronic component unless service manual specifically directs you to.

❑ Never work under a vehicle supported only by a jack.

❑ Cover all open fittings to avoid contamination from dirt or moisture.

❑ Handle components with care; avoid heat and liquids. Never weld near electronic parts.

❑ Never touch the computer input or output terminals; static discharge could destroy the ECM in an instant!

For specific information on wiring, component specifications, etc., refer to manufacturers' shop manuals.

Emission Systems Component Warranties

Most of the emission-control components are covered by a five-year/50,000-mile (whichever comes first) warranty against defects in materials and workmanship. Some OBD2 components are covered for eight years or 100,000 miles. Many people overlook this coverage, which is available at any franchised dealer. Federal regulations require the vehicle manufacturer (for example, Chrysler, Ford, General Motors, etc.) to provide this warranty to the original and subsequent owners of the vehicle.

These warranties generally include all of the major (expensive) parts of the fuel-injection and emission-control systems. Limited diagnostic time may also be included. Certain items, such as filters, are considered owner-maintenance items and are not covered.

Components damaged due to modification, abuse, or improper service procedures are also not covered. Refer to your vehicle owner's manual or your dealer for specific details.

Electronic engine-control systems are made up of large numbers of components. Knowing the functions of the various parts helps one understand how the entire system works and where to look when a problem arises. We have listed the major components used in domestic light-truck electronic-fuel systems. The descriptions in this chapter are necessarily generic in nature since not all fuel systems use all of the items listed here. However, they are representative of the majority of the systems used in domestic trucks and vans.

COMPUTER-CONTROLLED CARBURETORS

Carburetors rely on the difference between atmospheric pressure and the lower pressure (or so-called partial vacuum) inside the intake manifold to meter and atomize fuel. From the late 1970s through the late 1980s, many cars and light trucks used computer-controlled carburetors to reduce exhaust emissions. These systems used a fairly conventional carburetor, with the notable exception that it had a fuel-mixture solenoid. The computer would vary the engine's fuel mixture with this solenoid, based on information from the oxygen sensor.

When the engine warms up, the solenoid should make a buzzing sound that indicates that it's getting a signal and that it's working. These systems were an interim measure between the conventional carburetor and the feedback-type fuel-injection system.

FUEL INJECTION

Fuel injection, a system designed to meter the correct amounts of fuel into the engine during varying modes of operation, has been with us for a long time. In fact, airplanes have been equipped with it since the dawn of aviation with the Wright brothers in 1903. These early systems were rather crude, mechanically controlled devices. With the advent of solid-state electronics, electrons and transistors have taken over the job.

Electronically controlled fuel injection has gradually replaced carburetion and mechanical fuel injection as the system of choice because of its greater precision in providing the correct ratios of fuel and air under a wide variety of operating conditions. Engines will run on a wide range of air-fuel ratios, varying from about 8:1 to 20:1 by weight. However, the ideal (stoichiometric, for you chemistry buffs) mixture for low emissions is about 14.7 pounds of air for every pound of gasoline. Any more or less than this and emissions rise substantially.

TIPS THAT WORK

Shade-Tree Secret

When either lack of room or engine heat makes it hard to thread a spark plug into place, try putting a piece of rubber (or vinyl) hose on the end of the plug. When the plug tightens up, the hose slips and then can be easily removed. Finish tightening the spark plug as usual.

Larry Tudor, Norwalk, California

How Does Fuel Injection Work?

Fuel-injection sprays (injects) fuel under pressure into the airstream entering the engine, hence its name. Manufacturers use various types of fuel injection; however, the popular types all have much in common. Each uses a number of sensors to determine the operating conditions of the engine. A computer receives the signals from the various sensors and tells the fuel injectors how much fuel to spray and switches power to actuators that operate emission-control functions like exhaust gas recirculation and canister purge valves.

As the driver steps on the accelerator pedal, throttle plates in the throttle body open, allowing additional air to enter the intake manifold. As the air rushes into the manifold, the inside air pressure changes. Sensors detect this change instantly and pass the information on to the computer. When the computer gets the signals, it orders the fuel injectors to spray more fuel.

The first electronic systems in the late 1950s through the late 1970s metered the fuel much like the current ones, but they didn't monitor the exhaust. Increasingly stringent emission and fuel-economy regulations have prompted the vehicle manufacturers to introduce computer-controlled feedback systems, first on cars (most 1980 models had them) and later on light trucks, sport utility vehicles (SUVs), and vans. These systems use oxygen sensors to sniff the exhaust and tell the computer whether the fuel-metering program has missed the mark and the engine needs more or less fuel for a certain amount of air. Many of the early feedback systems used computer-controlled carburetors.

Think of an electronically controlled feedback fuel-delivery system as a circle or loop. When the engine is started, the oxygen sensor in the exhaust is cold and therefore unable to tell the computer what is happening. The engine runs on preset mixture values in the computer's memory. This condition is known as open loop because the circle is incomplete.

When the engine warms up to normal temperature, the oxygen sensor starts working (at about 600°F tip temperature), and the circle is completed. The computer uses the information from the oxygen sensor(s) to constantly adjust the fuel mixture. This is known as closed loop.

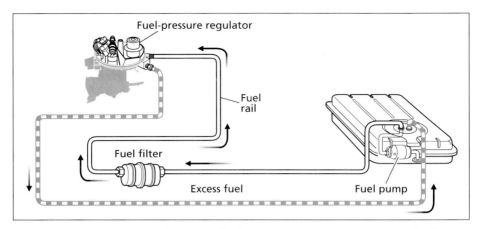

Figure 8.1: In single-point electronic fuel injection, used on vehicles in the late 1980s and early 1990s, fuel is injected at a throttle body on the intake manifold. Excess fuel is returned to the tank.

In the exhaust, the oxygen sensor(s) sniff, and if they find less oxygen (because a rich fuel mixture used it up), the computer uses this information to decide to cut back on the amount of fuel being sprayed into the engine.

This monitoring occurs rapidly and constantly. Each time the oxygen sensor detects a rich fuel mixture, it signals the computer to reduce the amount of fuel being injected. Corrections occur many times per second, allowing very accurate control of fuel flow. This precise metering is necessary to allow reduction-type catalytic converters to work efficiently in ridding the exhaust of oxides of nitrogen, carbon monoxide, and unburned hydrocarbons.

Throttle-Body Versus Port-Type Fuel Injection

Two basic fuel-injection designs are commonly used on domestic cars, light trucks, SUVs, and vans:

1. Throttle-body (or single-point or central) fuel injection *(Figure 8.1)*
2. Port-type (also called multi-port or multi-point) fuel injection *(Figure 8.2)*

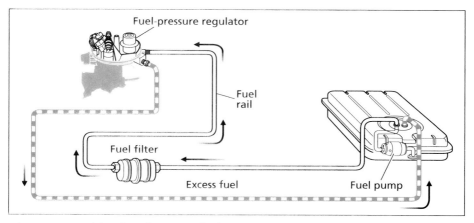

Fuel-pressure regulator

Fuel
rail

Fuel filter

Excess fuel   Fuel pump

Figure 8.2: Multi-point electronic fuel injection allows precise metering of fuel at each cylinder.

Both types work on the same basic principles. However, throttle-body systems more closely resemble carburetors in appearance and function, with the fuel being mixed with air in the throttle bore.

Fuel-injection systems use two basic types of air-flow metering: speed-density and mass air. Speed-density systems rely on manifold pressure, air charge temperature, and barometric sensors to calculate the volume and density of air entering the engine. Mass air sensors typically use airflow over a hot wire to calculate air density and flow. Mass air systems are more accurate and are used exclusively in port-type injection systems.

Throttle-body injection (TBI) systems control the air-fuel mixture more accurately than carburetors, are less prone to injector clogging, and cost less initially than port-type injection. However, with carburetors and TBI systems, the inner cylinders tend to get more fuel than the outer ones. This imbalance results in higher fuel consumption and exhaust emissions. Engine designers tried to compensate by supplying the inner cylinders with extra fuel so that the outer ones don't starve and incur lean misfire. For these and other reasons, throttle-body systems were phased out of production.

Port-type fuel-injection systems spray fuel into the intake ports just upstream of the intake valves, making this system more efficient because each cylinder gets the same amount of fuel. The downside of port-type fuel injection is the higher cost and greater susceptibility to leaks and injector clogging. The smaller orifices (compared to throttle-body systems) may become partially clogged with fuel deposits, and the spray pattern slowly deteriorates, resulting in drivability problems. Port fuel-injection systems also have throttle bodies to control airflow; however, the fuel is not mixed with the air at that point.

ONBOARD COMPUTERS

The onboard computer is commonly called an electronic (or engine) control module (ECM) *(Figure 8.3)*. These computers are also variously known by acronyms such as powertrain control module (PCM) and Dodge calls one type a single module engine control (SMEC).

The computer is the brain of the engine control system. It is usually contained in a metal box located within the dash, behind a kick panel, under the driver's seat, or in a protected location in the engine compartment.

An ECM may go into a "limp-in" mode if the signals from certain critical sensors are outside of preset design parameters. In some cases the computer will substitute fixed average values and disregard the out-of-range information the faulty sensor provides. The "check engine" light will come on, and power may be reduced. Problems of this nature should be corrected as soon as possible.

Most intermittent problems are caused by loose or corroded connections or damaged wiring. The only way to locate such problems is to duplicate the conditions that caused the problem. Note any recent repairs or maintenance which may have disturbed connections. Computer control units don't fail very often. In fact, they are one of the least common causes of engine malfunction. Statistics show that if the computer lasts the first six months, it will probably outlast the vehicle. Since the computer rarely fails and you suspect it has, get a professional to check it before you buy a new one.

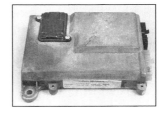

Figure 8.3:
The electronic control module (ECM) controls all aspects of engine operation and is located inside the vehicle or in a protected location under the hood.

Onboard Diagnostics

The first generation of electronic-feedback engine controls known as Onboard Diagnostics, Version 1, or OBD1, used oxygen sensors between the engine and the catalytic converter to monitor the fuel mixture and make running adjustments. These systems could only detect a limited number of malfunctions, like shorts or open circuits in the sensor and actuator circuits. They usually could not pinpoint the problem to a certain wire or sensor, only the circuit as a whole.

As computerized engine and emission control systems continue to evolve and become more sophisticated, they've taken on control of more functions and provide more precise management. The latest generation of emission controls, Onboard Diagnostics, Version 2, or OBD2, as it's usually called, was developed to address some of the shortcomings of the previous systems. Vehicles with OBD2 were first sold to the public as early as 1994; during the 1995 model year coverage was extended. California required them starting in 1996, with the introduction in remaining states slated for 1997. Computerized engine controls have also brought with them a blizzard of acronyms and each manufacturer used its own, often different, names. OBD2 regulations also seek to standardize these acronyms.

Among the new features of OBD2 is its ability to monitor the effectiveness of the vehicle's emission system in reducing pollution. OBD2 goes a step further than OBD1 by utilizing additional oxygen sensors downstream of the catalytic converter. The computer compares the signals coming from the upstream and downstream sensors. If there is no significant difference between the two signals, it indicates that the catalyst is not functioning.

Extremely accurate crankshaft position sensors allow the OBD2 systems to provide misfire detection. It monitors the rate the crankshaft accelerates after each cylinder fires. If the crankshaft accelerates less from a particular cylinder, OBD2 detects this and sets a trouble code.

OBD2 also stores short- and long-term fuel-trim data. This means that a technician can see how the engine controls have been adapting to operating conditions and/or correcting for any malfunctions such as vacuum leaks. Late-model computers can also detect sensor readings that are out of range and ones that don't change readings as they should or when they should. They also can detect actuators that don't respond correctly.

Figure 8.4:
A sensor in the
engine's air
intake tract
monitors air
temperature.

On OBD1 systems, each manufacturer had its own, completely different, sets of trouble codes and methods of accessing them. With OBD2, all manufacturers are required to use a set of more than 100 standardized trouble codes produced by the Society of Automotive Engineers (SAE). In addition, manufacturers can use additional codes for items of equipment that are specific to that brand. Unfortunately, special scan tools are required for accessing OBD2 codes, which prevent the average do-it-yourselfer from reading and using them for diagnosis.

If a problem is detected, a trouble code is set in the computer's memory, and the malfunction indicator lamp will be activated.

Malfunction Indicator Lamp

The malfunction indicator lamp (MIL) is also variously known as the "check engine," "service engine soon," or "power loss" light. MILs, as this acronym suggests, illuminate when there is a malfunction. The light is connected to the vehicle's onboard computer and illuminates when one or more monitored functions are found to be outside of normal ranges. The light should also be activated briefly as a bulb check every time the engine is started.

If the problem goes away or is repaired, the computer is designed to shut off the lamp after a preset number of engine starts. Trouble codes can also be cleared by disconnecting the battery or removing the ECM fuse for several seconds. See pages 198–201 for a listing of trouble codes related to the check engine light for various vehicle brands.

When these lights stay on, owners often go scurrying through their operator's manual to find out what it means, only to be told to take the vehicle to a dealer. The books don't tell you whether it's safe to continue driving or if it's really necessary to tow it in. Generally, if the oil pressure and coolant temperature are within normal ranges and the engine isn't smoking, making unusual sounds, or running very rough, it's okay to limp in for service.

FUEL INJECTION COMPONENTS

Air Charge Temperature Sensor

The Air Charge Temperature (ACT) sensor *(Figure 7.4)* measures the temperature of air entering the engine. This sensor allows the computer to make minor adjustments to fuel mixture and ignition timing due to changes in the temperature of the air.

Barometric-Pressure Sensor

Weather and altitude (air density) changes require alterations in fuel mixture. The barometric-pressure sensor is used on some systems to inform the computer of changes in ambient air pressure so adjustments can be made to compensate for air density.

Camshaft-Position Sensor

Camshaft-position sensors measure the angular position of the camshaft. The ECM uses this information along with CAS readings to determine if a particular cylinder is on compression or exhaust stroke.

Crankshaft-Angle Sensor

A crankshaft angle sensor (CAS) measures the angular position of the crankshaft. The ECM uses this information to determine when to spray fuel (on sequential port injection only), when to fire spark plugs, and when to detect misfire (OBD2 only). These sensors are mounted low on the engine and are prone to damage from road debris, water, and corrosion. Also, the wires and connections often get damaged or corroded. Owners can unplug and clean these terminals if a problem is suspected.

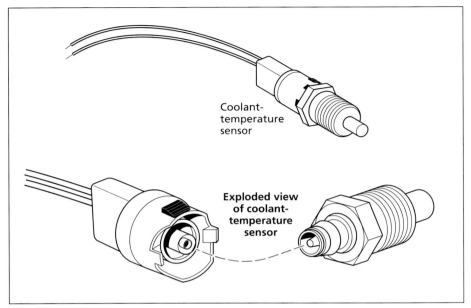

Coolant-
temperature
sensor

**Exploded view
of coolant-
temperature
sensor**

Figure 8.5: The electronic control system uses signals from the coolant temperature sensor to create proper air/fuel ratios for engine warmup.

Coolant-Temperature Sensor

The coolant-temperature sensor (CTS) is a temperature- sensing
resistor (thermistor) *(Figure 8.5)*. It is usually located in the intake
manifold near the thermostat, is screwed into a coolant passage, and
has two wires connected to it. Essentially, the CTS exists because cold
engines need more fuel than warm ones. The CTS tells the computer
how cold (or warm) the engine is by changing resistance as the
engine-coolant temperature changes. As the temperature goes down,
resistance goes up. The computer uses the CTS readings to lengthen
the "open" time of the injectors for a cold engine, which enriches the
fuel mixture like a choke does on a carbureted engine. When the
engine warms up, the fuel mixture is leaned out for best fuel economy
and low emissions.

Detonation Sensor

The detonation (knock) sensor converts mechanical energy (vibration) into electrical signals *(Figure 8.6)*. When the engine starts to

knock or "ping," this block-mounted sensor generates a small voltage signal that tells the computer to retard the ignition timing and/or enrich the fuel mixture until the knock goes away. Then it will gradually return to the original setting until the sensor once again detects knock or pinging. To check its operation, connect a timing light and, with the engine running, tap on the engine block with a hammer. If the timing retards, the knock sensor is working.

Figure 8.6: A detonation sensor monitors the engine for spark-knock ("ping") and reduces spark advance as necessary.

Electric Fuel Pump

Most electronically controlled fuel-injection systems have an electric fuel pump *(Figure 8.7)* mounted inside the fuel tank, combined with the sending unit for the fuel gauge. Tank-mounting the fuel pump reduces vapor lock tendency by pressurizing the entire fuel system. Additional pressure raises the vaporization point of the fuel. Some vehicles have an additional pump mounted on the chassis between the tank and engine.

If the engine won't start but has good spark, check the sound of the fuel pump. Listen for the characteristic whirring noise near the fuel tank while an assistant operates the starter. Remove the gas-filler cap to hear better, if necessary.

If the fuel pump doesn't run, check for voltage at the pump's electrical terminals while the engine is cranking. Also check the fuse, the inertia switch (if so equipped), and the relay(s) before you replace the fuel pump.

If your vehicle seems to be starving for fuel (surging, bucking, backfiring, etc.) or seems to be getting too much fuel (black, sooty spark-plug tips and/or exhaust, poor fuel mileage, etc.), perform a fuel-pressure test.

Figure 8.7: The electric fuel pump creates pressure from 9 to 45 psi, depending on design of the system.

Figure 8.8: When the ECM sends a voltage signal to the fuel injector, a solenoid inside the injector opens a path for the pressurized fuel to spray into the engine.

Always double-check the fuel level by thumping on the bottom of the tank(s)!

On Dodge and General Motors throttle-body systems, connect a T-fitting into the fuel line going to the throttle body (the one with the filter). Don't connect it to the return line; you'll get a false reading.

On all Ford EFI systems and later Dodge and GM port injection, connect the gauge to the pressure-checking port on the fuel-injector rail. These ports appear similar to Shrader-type tire valves with dust caps; you must have the right fittings for them. Use a gauge designed for fuel-pressure testing that has a rating higher than the maximum pressure specified for your engine. Dodge TBI calls for 14.5 psi fuel pressure, most Ford port injection allows a range from 35 to 45 psi, and GM TBI requires 9 to 13 psi. GM central multi-point injection used on light trucks up to 1995 operates at 58 to 64 psi. GM central sequential system used on Vortec engines starting in 1996 operate at 55 to 61 psi. The Dodge port injection typically uses 35 to 45 psi.

If the pressure is too high, check for a restricted return line. If the return line is open and unrestricted, replace the fuel-pressure regulator.

If the pressure is too low, look for a restricted line, hose, or fuel filter (don't forget the one in the tank). The fuel-pressure regulator could also be at fault. Momentarily pinch the fuel-return hose where it runs between the engine and frame. If the pressure rises rapidly, the regulator is probably bad. If the pressure doesn't rise with this test, the fuel pump is probably faulty.

Fuel Injectors

Fuel injectors are basically spray nozzles with electric solenoid-operated pintle valves *(Figure 8.8)*. When the computer sends a ground signal to the fuel injector, the solenoid opens a path for the pressurized fuel to spray into the engine. When the current flow is shut off, the fuel flow is shut off.

Throttle-body injectors can be checked quickly by removing the air cleaner and looking at the injectors while an assistant turns the ignition key to "on" and cranks the engine. Fuel should spray out. If it doesn't, disconnect the wiring harness from the injectors and connect a common 12-volt DC test light (or special "noid-light" tester) to the terminals. The light should pulse when the key is turned on. This means the electrical portion of the system is working. A steady light or no light indicates electrical malfunctions.

Port-type fuel injectors can be electrically checked in a similar manner. However, you can't view the fuel spraying out as you can on a throttle body. Instead, remove a spark plug to see if it is dry or wet with fuel.

Specially formulated fuel detergents have been added to most brands of gasoline to combat deposit formation, and nozzle designs have been changed to resist the tendency to clog. Several companies sell gasoline additives for your fuel tank that claim will unclog injectors. If all else fails, many repair shops have special injector-cleaning devices that chemically clean the nozzles on the vehicle. If you suspect that your engine is running rough because the injectors are clogged, have them cleaned and tested rather than replaced. Your wallet will thank you.

Fuel Filter

On fuel-injected vehicles, the fuel filter is important because the system is so sensitive to dirt and water *(Figure 8.9)*. The slightest speck of dirt can plug an injector nozzle. The fuel filter is usually located under the vehicle along the inside of a frame rail near the fuel tank. Most manufacturers recommend filter replacement at least every 30,000 miles; however, towing is considered "severe-duty" operation and requires more frequent replacement.

Warning: The fuel system is under pressure, even when the engine is not running! Read the precautions in this chapter, and follow the procedure for relieving fuel pressure before loosening any lines. Always use the exact replacement filter; don't risk a fire by using a substitute.

When loosening fuel lines with threaded fittings at either end of the filter, use the proper line wrenches to avoid rounding off the hex shapes and use a backup wrench to prevent twisting the fuel line.

Figure 8.9:
Effective fuel
filtration is
essential for
the close
tolerances
inside a fuel-
injection
system.

Figure 8.9: Effective fuel filtration is essential for the close tolerances inside a fuel-injection system.

Pour the contents of the old filter from the filter inlet into a clean container (not glass) and check for water and other contamination. Note the arrow on the filter, which indicates the direction of fuel flow, and always check for leaks after startup.

Fuel-Pressure Regulator

The fuel-pressure regulator *(Figure 8.10)* keeps the fuel at a preset constant pressure to prevent fluctuations in the fuel mixture that would change the mixture. The regulator maintains a constant pressure by returning the excess fuel to the fuel tank.

On Dodge and General Motors vehicles with TBI, the regulator is mounted in the throttle body; on Fords and other port-injected engines, the regulator is usually mounted at the downstream end of the fuel-injector rail. Some Chrysler models beginning in the mid 1990s have fuel systems with no returns—a single fuel line going to the engine. On these, the regulator is at the tank.

On most port-injected vehicles, the fuel-pressure regulator has another function. Since fuel is sprayed into the intake manifold (or ports), a substantial difference between pressure at the ports and in the intake manifold must be maintained. This is accomplished with a vacuum line that connects the regulator to a source of intake manifold vacuum to compensate for the changes in manifold pressure due to engine load. This diaphragm may be checked with a hand-pump vacuum tester. Replace the unit if it won't hold vacuum.

Idle Air-Control Valve

The idle air-control valve (IAC) is a computer-controlled air bypass that allows the computer to adjust idle speed to a predetermined rpm. It consists of an electric motor connected to a variable orifice. The IAC increases the size of the air passage to raise the idle in response to signals from the computer. This occurs, for example, when the engine is cold, the automatic transmission is put in gear, or the air conditioning is switched on.

Idle speed is computer controlled and is not usually adjustable. If the idle speed is too fast, check for vacuum leaks around the intake manifold, leaking hoses, and throttle-body base gaskets.

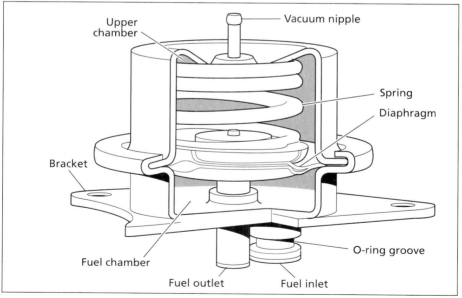

Figure 8.10: A fuel-pressure regulator maintains a specific pressure at the injectors and allows excess fuel to return to the tank.

Inertia Switch

The inertia switch shuts off the fuel pump in the event of an accident *(Figure 8.11)*. Whenever the fuel pump is inoperative, the inertia switch (if equipped) should be checked and reset if necessary. See your owner's manual for procedure and switch location.

Manifold Absolute-Pressure Sensor

Manifold absolute-pressure sensor (MAP) keeps the computer informed of changes in intake manifold pressure (partial vacuum) by varying resistance in relation to changes in pressure in the manifold. As engine load increases, the manifold pressure increases (or conversely, vacuum decreases).

Manifold Air-Temperature Sensor

The manifold air-temperature sensor (MAT) sensor (also known as the air-charge temperature [ACT] sensor) monitors the temperature of the air coming into the intake manifold. Colder air is more dense and requires more fuel than hot air. Since the MAT sensor is a thermistor (resistance varies with temperature), it alters the voltage signal going to the computer in relation to the temperature of the incoming air.

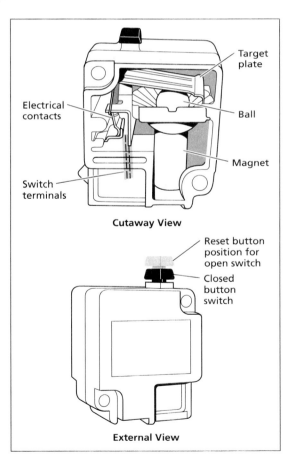

Cutaway View

External View

Figure 8.11: The inertia switch senses vehicle impact in an accident and shuts off the fuel pump to lower fire danger.

Oxygen Sensor

Oxygen (02) sensors allow the computer to know what is coming out the exhaust and to make corrections based on that information *(Figure 8.12)*. Every feedback or closed-loop system must have one.

Oxygen sensors are readily identified. They have a base similar in appearance to a spark plug and screw into the exhaust manifold or the exhaust pipe downstream of the manifolds. Earlier sensors are connected to only one wire; later models have two additional wires for a heating element that gets them working more quickly.

A zirconium element produces a small voltage in the presence of oxygen in the exhaust. This voltage, which will vary from 0 to 0.9 volts, with 0.450 volts indicating an ideal fuel mixture of 14.7:1, can be measured with an oxygen-sensor tester, or in some cases with a digital voltmeter probe inserted into the back of the oxygen-sensor connector. The voltage should constantly and rapidly vary with the engine running; if it doesn't, replace the sensor.

Figure 8.12: The oxygen sensor, mounted in the exhaust pipe, relays data to the computer for control of combustion.

Most oxygen sensors require replacement every 30,000 to 50,000 miles. They are easily replaced, and you can save a considerable amount of money by doing it yourself. Be sure the threads are coated with an anti-seize compound (Loctite 771-64 or equivalent); the compound usually is applied to new sensors by the manufacturer. Refer to your owner's manual for the replacement interval recommended by the manufacturer of your vehicle.

Some vehicles have more than one oxygen sensor; V-type engines may have one in each bank. Beginning with some 1995 models with OBD2 emission systems, there are also oxygen sensors downstream of the catalytic converters.

Note: Oxygen sensors may be ruined by the use of certain automotive silicone sealers; read the labels to determine if they are compatible with oxygen sensors.

Throttle-Position Sensor

Throttle-position sensors (TPS) tell the computer the rate of throttle opening and how far the throttle is open; they work by changing resistance as the throttle opens and closes. This allows the computer to enrich the fuel mixture when the throttle is opened suddenly, preventing hesitation.

The most common symptom of a faulty TPS is hesitation when the throttle is opened quickly. Two quick checks may be made with a digital voltmeter. With the ignition on:

1. Test for a reference voltage at the TPS (usually 5 volts). If voltage isn't present, trace and repair the wiring.
2. Check for a smooth voltage change as the throttle is opened and closed. If the voltage changes abruptly and unevenly, the TPS is probably faulty.

The initial (or base) setting of the TPS is also critical for good performance. Normally the TPS doesn't require adjustment. However, whenever it is replaced or when diagnosis indicates a problem, an adjustment should be performed following the factory-recommended procedure exactly. Since special tools are needed that are beyond the scope of the home mechanic, have this work done by a dealer or fuel-injection specialist.

Figure 8.13: The amount of airflow entering the engine is measured by the vane air-flow meter.

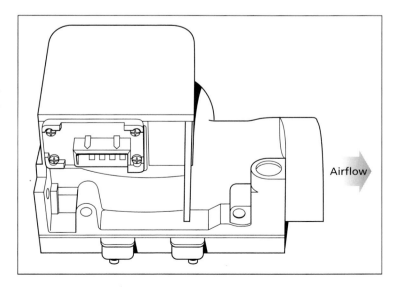

Airflow

Mass Airflow Sensor

Mass airflow (MAF) sensors indirectly measure the mass of air entering the engine. These units, noted for their precision, are mounted in the intake tract between the air filter and throttle body. Typically, MAF sensors use the cooling effect of air flowing over a heated wire to calculate the mass of air flowing through them.

Faulty MAFs may cause drivability problems like hesitation and backfiring, or may prevent the engine from running. The most effective way to test a MAF is with an oscilloscope, using a printed-scope pattern from a known good unit for comparison. A scan tool can also be used to check a MAF. However, here's one field test for a suspect MAF that is still functioning somewhat: Carefully check electrical connections, then tap on the housing of the MAF while the engine is idling. If the engine "coughs," replace the MAF.

Vane Airflow Meter

The vane airflow meter (VAF), used on certain port-type systems (some Ford trucks) only, measures the flow of air into the engine with an internal flap connected to a potentiometer (or variable resistor) *(Figure 8.13)*. Air temperature is also monitored by a built-in sensor.

The VAF meter is mounted between the throttle-control valve (or throttle body) and the air cleaner. A reference voltage is sent through the potentiometer and back to the computer. When the driver depresses the accelerator pedal, the increased volume of air entering the engine forces the flap to open wider, thus changing the resistance. The computer uses this information in determining how much fuel the engine needs.

Vehicle-Speed Sensor

Most computer-equipped vehicles are equipped with vehicle-speed sensors (VSS) that tell the computer how fast the vehicle is going. These sensors are usually mounted in the tailshaft of the transmission (or transfer case of 4WD models). When the vehicle is moving, a pulsing signal is generated. The computer uses the information provided by the speed sensor to control functions such as shift points and torque-converter lockup (on automatic transmission-equipped vehicles). The vehicle-speed sensors can be easily tested with a scan tool.

GENERAL MOTORS TROUBLE CODES

Code 12 Diagnostic mode
Code 13 Oxygen sensor or circuit
Code 14 Coolant sensor or circuit/high temperature indicated
Code 15 Coolant sensor or circuit/low temperature indicated
Code 16 System voltage high/ECM voltage over 17.1 volts
          (could be alternator problem)
Code 16 Distributorless Ignition System (DIS) circuit (Chevrolet cars only)
Code 17 Crank signal circuit (shorted) or faulty ECM
Code 18 Crank signal circuit (open) or faulty ECM
Code 19 Fuel pump circuit (shorted)
Code 20 Fuel pump circuit (open)
Code 21 Throttle Position Sensor (TPS) circuit or plunger
Code 22 Throttle Position Sensor (TPS) out of adjustment
Code 23 Mixture Control (MC) solenoid circuit (carbureted models)
Code 23 Manifold Absolute Temperature (MAT) sensor or circuit
          (fuel-injected models) low temperature indicated
Code 23 Electronic Spark Timing (EST) bypass circuit problem
          (Cadillac DFI models)
Code 24 Vehicle Speed Sensor (VSI) or circuit
Code 25 Manifold Air Temperature (MAT) sensor or circuit
          (high temperature indicated)
Code 25 Modulated displacement failure (1981 Cadillac V8, V6, V4 only)
Code 25 Electronic Spark Timing (EST) (Cadillac HT4100 only)
Code 26 Quad Driver Circuit (dealer serviced)
Code 26 Throttle switch circuit shorted
Code 27 Throttle switch circuit open
Code 27 Gear Switch Diagnosis (dealer serviced)
Code 28 Pressure Switch Manifold check (PSM) vehicles with
          4L80-E transmissions
Code 28 Same as Code 27
Code 29 Same as Code 27
Code 31 Turbo overboost (turbo models only)
Code 31 Park/Neutral Switch (3.3L V6)
Code 31 Manifold Air Temperature (MAT)   sensor or circuit
          (Cadillac DFI models)
Code 31 Canister purge solenoid circuit
Code 31 Camshaft sensor or circuit
Code 32 BARO sensor or circuit (carbureted models)
Code 32 EGR circuit (fuel-injected models)
Code 32 Digital EGR circuit (3.1L V6)
Code 33 Manifold Absolute Pressure (MAP) sensor or circuit (low vacuum)
Code 33 Mass Air Flow (MAF) sensor or circuit
Code 34 Mass Air Flow (MAF) sensor or circuit
Code 34 Vacuum sensor or Manifold Absolute Pressure (MAP) sensor
          (high vacuum) or circuit

GENERAL MOTORS TROUBLE CODES continued

Code 35	Idle Air Control (IAC) valve or circuit
Code 35	Idle Speed Control (ISC) switch or circuit (shorted)
Code 35	BARO sensor or circuit shorted (Cadillac DFI models)
Code 36	BARO sensor or circuit open (Cadillac DFI models)
Code 36	Mass Air Flow (MAF) sensor burn-off circuit
Code 36	Distributorless Ignition System (DIS) (Quad-4)
Code 37	Manifold Absolute Temperature (MAT) sensor or circuit shorted (Cadillac HT4100)
Code 38	Manifold Absolute Temperature (MAT) sensor or circuit open (Cadillac HT4100)
Code 38	Brake Input Circuit (brake light switch)
Code 39	Torque Converter Clutch (TCC)
Code 41	No distributor signals to ECM, or faulty ignition module
Code 41	Cam sensors or circuit
Code 41	Cylinder select error
Code 41	Quad-4 engine 1X reference (check ignition module/ECM)
Code 42	Electronic Spark Timing (EST) circuit
Code 43	Electronic Spark Control (ESC) unit
Code 43	Throttle Position (TPS) out of adjustment
Code 44	Oxygen sensor or circuit—lean exhaust
Code 45	Oxygen sensor or circuit—rich exhaust
Code 46	Power steering pressure switch (4-cylnder air-conditioned models)
Code 46	Vehicle Anti-Theft System (VATS)
Code 44	Oxygen sensor or circuit—lean exhaust
Code 48	Misfire diagnosis
Code 51	PROM, MEM-CAL, or ECM problem
Code 52	CALPAK or ECM problem
Code 53	System over-voltage (ECM) over 17.7 volts)
Code 53	EGR system (carbureted models)
Code 53	Distributor signal interrupt (1983 and later Cadillac HT4100)
Code 53	Alternator voltage out of range
Code 54	Mixture control (M/C) solenoid or ECM (carbureted models)
Code 54	Fuel pump circuit (fuel-injected models)
Code 55	Oxygen sensor circuit (ECM
Code 56	Vacuum sensor circuit
Code 61	Oxygen sensor signal faulty
Code 62	Transaxle gear switch signal circuits (3.1L V6/Quad-4 engines)
Code 62	Engine oil temperature sensor
Code 63	EGR flow check
Code 64	Same as Code 63
Code 65	Same as Code 63
Code 65	Fuel Injection Circuit (Quad-4 engines)
Code 66	Air-conditioning pressure sensor circuit

CHRYSLER MOTORS TROUBLE CODES

Code 11	Engine not cranked since battery was disconnected/no distributor input signal
Code 12	Memory standby power lost
Code 13*	Manifold Absolute Pressure (MAP) sensor vacuum circuit
Code 14*	Manifold Absolute Pressure (MAP) sensor electrical circuit
Code 15**	Vehicle speed/distance circuit
Code 16*	Loss of battery voltage
Code 17	Engine running too cold
Code 21*	Oxygen sensor circuit
Code 19	Fuel pump circuit (shorted)
Code 20	Fuel pump circuit (open)
Code 22*	Coolant temperature sensor unit
Code 23	Throttle body temperature sensor circuit
Code 24*	Throttle position sensor circuit
Code 25**	Idle Speed Control (EST) motor-driver circuit
Code 25	Automatic Idle Speed (AIS) motor driver circuit
Code 26*	Peak injector current has not been reached or injector circuits have high resistance
Code 27*	Fuel Injector Control circuit/or injector output circuit not responding
Code 31**	Canister purge solenoid circuit failure
Code 32**	Exhaust Gas Recirculation (EGR) system failure/power loss light circuit (some 1987 models)
Code 33	A/C clutch cutout relay circuit
Code 34	Speed control vacuum or vent control solenoid circuits/an open or shorted circuit at the EGR solenoid (1987 models)
Code 35	Idle switch circuit/cooling fan relay circuit
Code 36*	Air switching solenoid circuit (non turbo) or wastegate solenoid circuit on tubocharged models
Code 37	Part throttle unlock solenoid driver circuit (automatic transmission only) or shift indicator light circuit (lockup converter
Code 41	Charging system excess or lack of field current
Code 42	Automatic Shutdown relay driver circuit (ASD)
Code 43	Ignition coil control circuit/or spark interface circuit
Code 44	Loss of FJ2 to logic board/battery temperature out of range (1987) or failure in the SMEC/SBEC
Code 45	Overboost shut-off circuit (1987) on MAP sensor reading above overboost limit detected/overdrive solenoid (A-500 or A-518 automatic transmission)
Code 46*	Battery voltage too high
Code 47	Battery voltage too low
Code 51**	Oxygen sensor indicates lean
Code 52*	Oxygen sensor indicates rich
Code 53	Module internal problem/SMEC/SBEC failure. Internal engine controller fault condition detected

CHRYSLER MOTORS TROUBLE CODES continued

Code 54   Problem with the distributor synchronization circuit
Code 55   End of code output
Code 61*   BARO solenoid failure
Code 62   Emissions reminder light mileage is not being updated
Code 63   EEPROM write denied/controller failure

  *These codes light up Check Engine light
**These codes light up Check Engine light on vehicles with special California
   emissions controls

DODGE TROUBLE CODES

Code 88   Start of test
Code 11   Engine not cranked since battery was disconnected
Code 12   Memory standby power lost
Code 13   MAP sensor pneumatic circuit
Code 14   MAP sensor electrical circuit
Code 15   Faulty vehicle distance sensor circuit (California only)
Code 16   Loss of battery voltage
Code 17   Engine temperature too low
Code 21   Oxygen-sensor circuit
Code 22   Coolant-temperature circuit
Code 23   Throttle-body temperature-sensor circuit
Code 24   Throttle-position sensor
Code 25   Idle speed-control circuit
Code 26   High resistance in injector circuit
Code 27   Fuel-injector control problem
Code 31   Vapor canister purge solenoid circuit
Code 32   Exhaust-gas recirculation valve circuit
Code 33   A/C cutout-relay circuit
Code 35   Idle switch circuit
Code 36   Air-switching solenoid circuit
Code 37   Part throttle unlock solenoiddriver circuit
           (automatic transmission only)
Code 41   Alternator field current
Code 42   Auto shutdown relay driver circuit
Code 43   Ignition coil-control circuit
Code 44   Loss of FJ2 to logic board
Code 46   High battery voltage
Code 47   Low battery voltage
Code 51   Lean oxygen-sensor signal
Code 52   Rich oxygen-sensor signal
Code 53   Internal module problem
Code 55   End of message

TROUBLE CODES

Dodge Trouble Codes

Fuel-injected Dodge trucks and vans prior to the introduction of the Magnum series engines use a throttle-body system. The computer (or SMEC) is usually located in the engine compartment adjacent to the left fender. Whenever the SMEC detects a problem, the "check engine" light on the dash is activated. This light may also be used as a diagnostic tool. By turning the ignition key on-off-on-off within five seconds (with the engine not running—do not activate the starter), electronically stored trouble codes may be accessed. The lamp should light for three seconds as a bulb check before displaying the trouble codes.

These codes are displayed as flashes of light. For example, Code 11 would appear as one blink, a short pause, another blink, then a long pause before the next code.

The computer will flash all codes stored in memory and then repeat them until the key is turned off. These codes represent problems detected by the computer in approximately the last fifty engine starts. **Note:** Missing code numbers are intentional by the manufacturer.

After repairs are made, disconnect the negative battery cable from the battery for five minutes to clear all stored codes. Reconnect the battery and drive the vehicle for about ten miles to allow the computer to relearn the engine's characteristics. The engine may run roughly after first starting up.

Ford EEC IV Trouble Codes

Ford trouble codes may be accessed with a special tester or an analog voltmeter. The procedures vary considerably with each engine option and model and are so complex that we recommend you take the vehicle to a qualified technician for these checks.

Before you throw in the towel, check all the usual problem areas we have listed. In addition, check the inertia switch, as this seems to be a common problem on Fords. Simply push the reset button as described in the owner's manual. The inertia switch on F-series trucks is beneath the dash behind the left kick panel. On E-series vans, the switch is located under the right side of the dash under the heater-blower register.

General Motors Fuel Injection

General Motors computer trouble codes are displayed by the "check engine" light in the instrument cluster. They may be accessed by switching the ignition on with the engine not running. The "check engine" lamp should light as a bulb check. Then locate the 12-pin Assembly Line Diagnostic Link (ALDL) under the driver's side of the dash. Bridge the "A" and "B" terminals together with a special key or, in a pinch, use a bent paper clip or a short piece of wire.

These codes are displayed as flashes of light. For example, Code 12 would appear as one blink, a short pause, two blinks, then a long pause before the next code. (Missing code numbers are intentional by the manufacturer.) The computer will flash all codes stored in memory three times each and then repeat them until the tool is removed from the ALDL. After repairs are made, disconnect the negative battery cable from the battery for five minutes to clear all stored codes. Reconnect the battery and drive the vehicle for about ten miles to allow the computer to relearn the engine's characteristics. The engine may run roughly at first. After testing, remove the bridging device from ALDL to exit code display mode.

"No-Code" Drivability Problems

Unfortunately, not all operational problems are covered by a trouble code, nor do problems always trigger a trouble code. These problems are called "no-code" drivability complaints. Such faults are more difficult to track down, because you don't have a clear-cut starting point as you do when a code is set. In these cases you have to use basic mechanical sleuthing, just as technicians always did before there were trouble codes.

There's a tendency with computer-controlled engines to assume that problems are usually in the computer or its circuitry. However, don't forget that there's an engine under all that stuff, with pistons, valves, and gaskets. Always check the basics first: filters, plugs, cap and rotor, and ignition cables. Look for vacuum hoses that are cracked or disconnected and wires/cables that may be chafed through or cut. Battery and charging problems can raise havoc. Use a digital voltmeter to test battery voltage when the engine is running. If all these check out, test compression and cylinder leakdown rate to ensure that the engine is in good mechanical condition.

From Samer's RV Kitchens

G ood Sam Club Members enjoy quick and easy "on the road" recipes. This special bonus chapter offers a unique collection of Appetizers from the RV Kitchens of Good Sam Club Members. You'll find delicious recipes with easy to follow instructions, along with equipment and ingredients that travel well in your RV. From Art's Salsa to Bill's Tangy Cheese-ball, to Spinach Tortilla Rollups, here are favorite recipes *Samers* love to serve.

"These are Different" Celery Sticks

1 large bunch celery
1 8-ounce package cream cheese
1 8½ ounce can crushed pineapples,
   well drained
½ cup chopped pecans
2 tablespoons finely chopped green peppers
1 tablespoon finely chopped onion
1½ teaspoons seasoned salt

Clean celery well. Cut each stick into 2½ - inch pieces. Mix together cream cheese, pineapple, nuts, green pepper, onion, and salt. Chill for several hours or overnight. Fill celery pieces with mixture and arrange on platter.

Donna Lee McKenna
Omaha, Nebraska
Bug N Sam

Serves 25

Oysterette Snacks

1 12-ounce box oysterette crackers
1 cup vegetable oil
1 4-ounce package ranch-style dressing mix
1/4 cup grated Parmesan cheese
1/2 teaspoon garlic powder
1/2 teaspoon dillweed

*P*lace crackers in large self-sealing plastic bag. Pour in oil and turn from side to side until all crackers are moistened. Mix dry ingredients together and pour into bag. Seal tightly and turn from side to side until crackers are coated with seasonings.

Irene L Tujague
Thousand Oaks, California
Past Presidents Sams

Serves 10

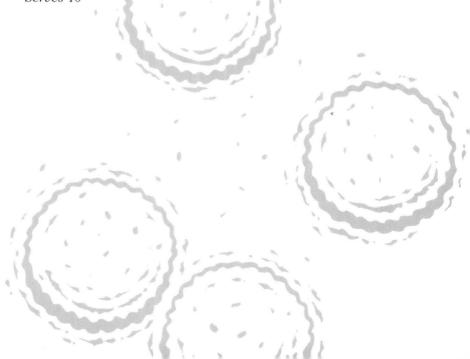

Spinach Tortilla Rollups

6 green onions, finely chopped
2 tablespoons finely chopped cilantro
    (optional)
1 tablespoon finely chopped parsley
1 3-ounce can real bacon bits
1 cup mayonnaise
1 cup sour cream
1 4-ounce package ranch style dressing mix
2 10-ounce packages chopped frozen
    spinach, thawed and dried
8 flour tortillas

In large bowl, mix onions, cilantro, parsley, bacon bits, mayonnaise, sour cream, and dressing mix. Tear spinach into pieces and add to mixture; mix well.

Spread ⅛ of mixture over each tortilla; rollup, leaving ends open. Slice into bite-size pieces before serving.
Hint: These are delicious when warm. Pop rollups into microwave oven to heat just before serving.

Sharon McConnell
Bonita, California
Sandpiper Sams

Serves 14

Happy Hour Special

1 11-ounce package refrigerator biscuits
½ cup butter or margarine
2 cloves garlic, crushed
1 tablespoon sesame seeds

*P*reheat oven to 375° F.
Cut biscuits into quarters and place in
11 × 7-inch baking pan. Melt butter and stir in
garlic. Pour over biscuit pieces, making certain
that all are well covered. Sprinkle with sesame
seeds. Bake 8 to 10 minutes or until biscuits
spring back when lightly touched. Serve warm.
*Hint: Parmesan cheese can be substituted for
sesame seeds.*

Shirley Jairell
Laramie, Wyoming
Gem City Sams

Serves 10

Hot and Hearty Beef and Bean Dip

1 pound lean ground beef
1 2-ounce can green chilies
½ large onion, chopped
1 16-ounce can refried beans
1 pound cheddar cheese, grated
4 ounces guacamole dip, mixed with
1 cup sour cream

Brown ground beef in 12-inch skillet with chilies and onion. Drain fat. In an 8×10 baking pan, layer refried beans, ground beef, and grated cheese. Bake 15 minutes.

Remove from oven and spread the guacamole-sour cream mixture over top of ground beef mixture. Serve with Mexican-style chips or crackers.

Betty Busse
Missoula, Montana
Garden City Sams

Serves 6 to 8

Spicy Pecans

1 pound pecans, shelled
½ cup margarine or butter, melted
Celery salt to taste
Garlic powder to taste, or 1 small clove garlic, minced
Cayenne pepper to taste
Salt and pepper to taste

Preheat oven to 200° F.
Toast the pecans on a baking sheet for 20 minutes, stirring every 5 to 10 minutes. Pour melted butter over pecans and toss thoroughly. Sprinkle on celery salt, garlic, cayenne, and salt and pepper to taste. Serve warm or at room temperature.

Alta McNutt
Sierra Vista, Arizona
Cockise Renegades

Serves 4 to 6

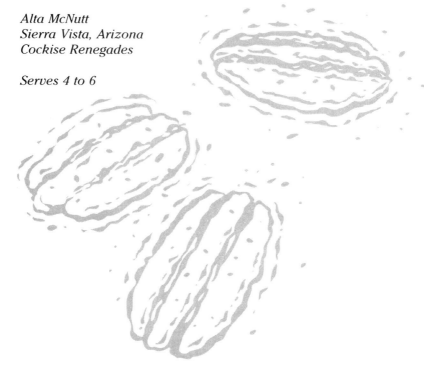

Art's Salsa

2 large bunches green onions, finely chopped
For milder flavor:
1 4-ounce can diced green chilies
For hotter flavor:
1 3½-ounce can diced jalapeno peppers
1 4½-ounce can chopped black olives
5 large tomatoes, diced
1 8-ounce bottle Italian salad dressing

Mix all ingredients in 1-quart bowl. Chill overnight.

Arthur Schaut, Jr.
Duarte, California
Semper Fi Sams

Makes 3 to 4 cups

Crabmeat Dip

1 8-ounce package cream cheese,
    room temperature
2 tablespoons mayonnaise
2 tablespoons Worcestershire sauce
1 teaspoon lemon juice
1 small onion, minced
½ 12-ounce bottle chili sauce
1 6-ounce package frozen crabmeat, thawed,
    or 1 6-ounce can crabmeat
Chopped parsley for garnish

Mix first 5 ingredients together. Place on serving platter or dip plate. Pour chili sauce over cream cheese mixture. Sprinkle crabmeat over mixture and top with chopped parsley. Chill well before serving.

Ruth Shake
Odon, Indiana
Cherokee Sams

Serves 8-10

Fiesta Dip

1 10½-ounce can bean dip
2 ripe avocados, peeled, pitted, and mashed
3 tablespoons mayonnaise
3 tablespoons sour cream
½ 1.25-ounce package taco seasoning mix
1 4¼-ounce can chopped black olives
1 bunch green onions, chopped,
   including tops
1½ cups grated cheddar cheese
2 large tomatoes, chopped
Salsa to taste

Spread bean dip over 12-inch serving plate. Combine avocados, mayonnaise, sour cream, and taco seasoning; blend well. Spread over bean dip. Layer with olives, onions, and cheese. Just before serving add tomatoes and sprinkle with salsa. Serve with taco chips.

Mildred Smith
Orange, California
Lucky 13

Serves 8

Jenny's Dip

1 8-ounce package cream cheese, room temperature
1 8-ounce carton sour cream
2 tablespoons milk
2 tablespoons minced bell pepper
2 tablespoons minced onion
1 2½-ounce jar or package chipped beef, minced

*H*ave all ingredients at room temperature before starting. Mix until well blended. Serve with raw vegetables for dipping.

Karen Fisk
Agoura, California
Member at Large

Serves 8

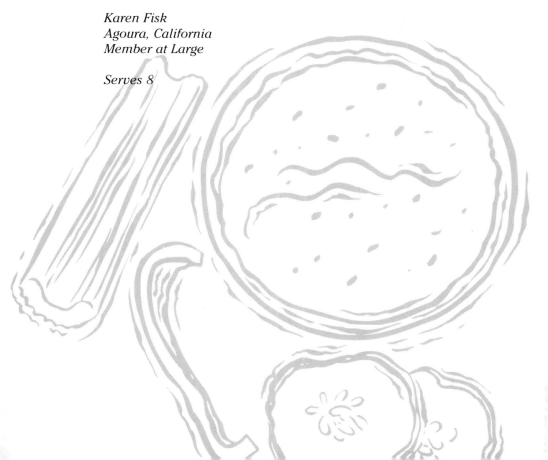

Bill's Tangy Cheese Ball

8-ounce package cream cheese, room
temperature
2 tablespoons dried green pepper flakes
½ cup sliced green olives with pimientos
½ cup diced black olives
1 tablespoon instant dried minced onions
2 teaspoons Tabasco sauce
½ cup dried parsley flakes

Blend cream cheese, green pepper, olives, onions, and Tabasco sauce with a fork in a medium-size bowl. Shape mixture into a round ball. Roll in parsley flakes until covered slightly, and refrigerate for at least 1 hour before serving. Present on platter surrounded with snack crackers.

Hint: This will keep in the refrigerator for up to 2 weeks. You can add fresh sprigs of parsley around base of ball for an added festive touch.

William Purkett
Havre, Montana
Milk River Sams

Jalapeno Jelly Camp-Out Dip

7 jalapeno peppers, roasted and peeled,
   seeds removed
   or 1 7-ounce can whole jalapeno peppers,
   seeds removed
1 green pepper, seeds removed,
   cut into squares
2 tablespoons fresh lemon juice
1½ cups cider vinegar
3½ cups sugar
1 6-ounce bottle liquid pectin
5 drops green food coloring
1 8-ounce package cream cheese

Mix all ingredients except sugar in blender and puree until smooth. Pour mixture into large saucepan and add sugar. Bring to boil and simmer 10 minutes. Remove pan from heat and add pectin and food coloring.

Divide into sterilized canning jars and seal. When ready to serve, pour one jar over cream cheese and accompany with crackers.

Lil Clark
Sparks, Nevada
Silver Sage Sams

Makes 4½ pints

Dee's Hot Cheese Dip

1 pound sharp cheddar cheese
1 pound processed cheese food spread
   (Velveeta)
1 16-ounce can whole tomatoes, well drained
2 4-ounce cans chopped green chilies, drained
1/4 teaspoon garlic powder

Cut cheeses into cubes and melt in crockpot or fondue pot. Cut up tomatoes and mix well with cheeses. Add chilies and garlic powder and stir gently until smooth. Heat until mixture is warm.

Dee Miller
Cape May, New Jersey
Cape May Diamonds

Hot Artichoke Dip

1 16-ounce can artichoke hearts in water,
    drained
1 6-ounce jar marinated artichoke hearts,
    drained
1 4-ounce can diced green chilies, drained
8 – 10 tablespoons mayonnaise
2 cups shredded sharp cheddar cheese

*P*reheat oven to 350° F.
Chop artichokes and mix both varieties
together. Place in shallow 2-quart baking dish or
8 × 8-inch pan. Sprinkle chilies over top. Spread
mayonnaise over entire dish to seal. Sprinkle
with shredded cheese. (Cover with plastic wrap
and refrigerate if making ahead.)

To bake, place in preheated oven for 20 minutes until hot and bubbly. Recipe also can be
microwaved on high 5 to 10 minutes. Serve with
assorted crackers.

Audrey Renish
Joshua Tree, California
Joshua Jacks Sams

Serves 8

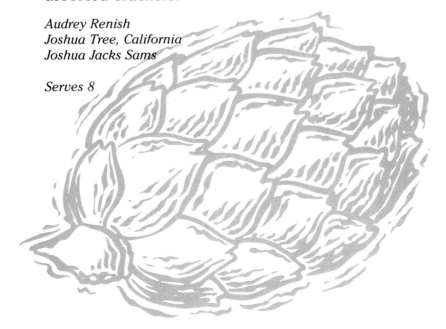

Index

Minneapolis
Mississippi
U. S. A.
L. Michi
Milwa
Chicago
aha
Kansas City
St. Louis
Louis
Missouri R.
Arkansas R.
Memphis
Mississippi R.
Mississippi
Birmin